HI THERE,
I JUST WANT YOU TO KNOW THAT
THIS IS NOT A LIBRARY PROPERTY
SO FEEL FREE TO TAKE IT FOR FREE
IF YOU WANT TO READ IT

PLEASE READ THE BACK TO SEE IF
ITS SOMETHING YOU WOULD WANT
TO READ OTHERWISE FEEL FREE TO
LEAVE IT TO SOMEONE WHO WANTS
TO READ IT

I, AN AUTHOR IS THE ONE
WHO PUT IT HERE
BECAUSE OF UNDER
CIRCUMSTANCES I CAN'T
THROW IT AWAY

American Asylee

Dedication

I dedicate this book to my mother, Ruta Teboitabu

A young Pacific Island woman's true coming-of-age story takes the reader from an endangered small island state to rural Philippine villages and ends in an American jail. She and other detainees share a life inside walls few have ever entered. Narratives of survival, rooted in faiths stronger than the concrete that incarcerates them, will shock, awe, and inspire the reader as the women wait for their cases to be heard. Icons for all domestic violence survivors, faith followers, and humanitarians working towards a more globally just society, these women are the faces of today's American asylees.

Contents

———— ★ ★ ★ ————

Setting

---- ★ ★ ★ ----

Kiribati

Aformer British colony, the Republic of Kiribati (Kee-ree-bas) became an independent nation on July 12, 1979. With a total land area of 811 km², the country comprises 32 coral atolls and one raised island. Its sovereign territory spreads across 3.5 million km² of the Central Pacific Ocean and holds the exclusive distinction of being the only country in all four quadrants of the Earth. The International Date Line and the Equator intersect in its territory, making it the first nation to greet each new day, month, year, and millennium. The result of global climate change is one of five endangered nations predicted to be uninhabitable within this century. With a nearly equivalent female-to-male ratio, the nation's population was estimated to be 116,000 in 2018.

Domestic violence has been commonplace for many women and families in Kiribati. According to a United Nations Women's prevalence of violence against women study, 68% of Kiribati women aged 15-49 have experienced physical and/or sexual intimate partner violence, and 36% have experienced physical and/or sexual intimate partner violence within the past 12 months. Ten percent have experienced sexual abuse by someone other than an intimate partner since age 15.[1] In 2018, 20% of women aged 20 to 24 were first married or in a union with a male partner before age 18.[2]

***

The United States of America

Since World War II, the United States has welcomed more refugees than any other country in the world. Historically, the U.S. refugee intake ceiling has hovered around 80,000 people per year. However, in 2017, the intake dropped to 50,000. In 2018, it fell to 45,000, and in 2019, it dropped to 30,000.[3] The Trump administration was

---

[1] Secretariat of the Pacific Community, 2010. Kiribati Family Health and Support Study: A study on violence against women and children. Noumea, New Caledonia.

[2] UNICEF global databases, 2018, based on Demographic and Health Surveys (DHS), Multiple Indicator Cluster Surveys (MICS) and other nationally representative surveys.

[3] U.S. Annual Refugee Resettlement Ceilings and Numbers of Refugees Admitted, 180-Present.

responsible for this downward trend, aiming to half the allotted number in 2020. Humanity faces a growing population displacement crisis, increasing international conflicts, and environmental catastrophes worldwide. Reducing US asylum intake numbers places hundreds of thousands in harm's way.

Recognizing this, the subsequent administration created the U.S. Citizenship Act of 2021. Signed on the first day of the Biden-Harris administration, the act sought to "restore humanity and American values to the immigration system" by creating new pathways to citizenship, strengthening labor protections, prioritizing smart border controls, and addressing root causes of migration. Specifically, for asylum seekers, the act "eliminates the one-year deadline for filing asylum claims and provides funding to reduce asylum application backlogs.[4]"

Three weeks after creating the U.S. Citizenship Act of 2021, the Biden-Harris administration signed the executive order on Rebuilding and Enhancing Programs to Resettle Refugees and Planning for the Impact of Climate Change on Migration. The order called for a report on the "international security implications of climate-related

---

[4] U.S. Citizenship Act of 2021

migration; options for protection and resettlement of individuals displaced directly or indirectly from climate change.

The executive order is in direct accord with 2021 reintroduced legislation by Representative Nydia M. Velázquez (NY-07) and Senator Edward J. Markey (D-Mass) to establish a national strategy for addressing global climate displaced individuals lacking any legal protection under international law.[5]

This act supports the UN human rights council's ruling stating that people seeking asylum through climate-related threats cannot be deported back to the countries they are fleeing. The committee rationalized this by seeing that climate-related events can occur both suddenly - such as intense storms or flooding - or over time through slow-onset processes such as sea-level rise and land degradation; either situation could spur people to seek safety elsewhere.[6]

The following narrative is a personal account of one I-Kiribati[7] woman's fight for safety, purpose, and acceptance in 2020's United States of America, a nation in

---

[5] Reintroduction of H.R.4732 and S.2565 (117th US Congress).

[6] UN News Kiribati (21 January 2020).

[7] Native term for individuals from The Nation of Kiribati.

recovery and largely divided on issues of migration, asylum, climate change, and social justice.

American Asylee

October 2015 - Abaiang, Kiribati

↓

November 2015 - Idaho, USA

↓

December 2015 - Utah, USA

↓

January 2016 - Los Angeles, USA

↓

February 2016 - London, United Kingdom

↓

March 2016 - Los Angeles, USA

↓

July 2016 - Sydney, Australia

↓

July 29, 2016 - Orange County Correctional Facility

↓

August 9, 2017 - San Pedro, California

↓

March 2019 - Inglewood, California

↓

April 14, 2022 – Los Angeles, California

Absence doesn't make the heart grow fonder

* ★ *

We met in 1999, during our first year of high school. Both of us came from different schools, and though we didn't hang out much, I felt so comfortable with him. I was living on the school's compound at the time. He was living with his family. We boarding students always asked those living at home for things like new books and invitations to family gatherings to make us feel better. That's how I came to know Tee. From a distance, Tee seemed like a terrible student. He seemed to have little interest in school and was always placed at the top of his class. People would go on about his intelligence, good looks, and personality, but I was too young back then to notice. Our friendship was like a brother-sister relationship. I was the little matchmaker for him and his friends. I knew about their crushes and all the girls who had crushes on them. The job wasn't always pleasant, but

I enjoyed it. Tee was expelled one year after beginning high school, and after that, we hardly saw each other.

A couple of years passed before we saw each other again. My friend would go to a nightclub to dance on the weekends, and that is where I saw Tee again. As my friend and I walked home, Tee walked up and talked to me. By the end of the walk, we were in a relationship. I was unsure what kind of a relationship, but we were in one.

We stayed in contact for the next few months until Tee disappeared. No more calling, visiting, or any kind of close contact. It was like I had been dropped from a cliff without warning. When we would be in the same vicinity and make eye contact, he would hide. Eventually, I learned that he was in a new relationship. I was devastated. The worst part was not knowing where it all went wrong. I went crazy, thinking that I still had a chance with him, somehow hoping he would come back.

I began spending time with my friends and family, doing all I could to keep my mind off him. Eventually, in large part, due to a newfound faith in the Church of Jesus Christ of Latter-day Saints, I began to enjoy life without him. I began to smile again, and eventually, time passed without a single thought of him.

Nightclubs were replaced with church activities, old friends were replaced with new friends, old ways were replaced with new ways, and an old life was replaced with a new life. Raised Roman Catholic, my mother was against my new faith. For weeks, she refused to speak to me. It was hard because we were very close to each other. Eventually, when she realized the positive influence my new faith had on my life, she began to appreciate the new me. Our relationship mended, and things eventually returned to the way they were before.

Months passed before I even began thinking about dancing again. I did so when asked to perform at a wedding. My cousins and I spent weeks practicing three songs for the wedding. After our performance, we went outside to wind down. Outside, Tee's best friend approached me and asked if he could talk to me. Initially, I wanted nothing to do with him. He hurt me, and I moved on. I didn't want to reopen old wounds. But I said yes. This time, I thought, I'll make sure he falls in love with me and then break his heart, so he knows how it feels. That night, our relationship resumed. Days turned into weeks, and weeks turned into months. Tee was different. He was better. Was this the same man I planned to dump?

We started hanging out with his friends, and he began taking me out in public. I found myself falling in love all over again. With all his changes and the respect he showed me, I couldn't help but want him in my life again. Revenge wasn't my motive any longer. I loved who he was and who I was with. Time with him was filled with purpose and love, and finally, we became a real couple.

One night we went to the cinema with a group of friends. While waiting, a friend questioned Tee about our future. "How are you going to survive? Everyone knows Grace is lazy." Of course, we all laughed, but deep down, I was hurt. "That's not a problem," Tee replied, "we will hire someone to clean for us." Having his support meant everything to me. He knew my shortcomings and still saw me as perfect for him.

***

The hardest part of our relationship was during my first year of university studies in Fiji. We had been separated for over a year when he won a scholarship to an Australian University. I remember teasing him when learning. He spent the entire day in his room, crying, after dropping me off at the airport. I had always been the one to leave for my studies previously. This was different. Now knowing how it felt to be left behind, I regretted teasing him in the first place.

Before boarding, he handed me a CD wrapped in a letter. Thinking his words would somehow relieve me of my pain, I opened the letter and read:

Dear Grace,

Inside this letter is a CD with one song called, "If You're Not the One." Every time I hear it, it reminds me of you. I hope one day it will remind you of me as well. As you listen, pretend that I am the one singing these words to you:

If you're not the one, then why does my soul feel glad today? If you're not the one, then why does my hand fit yours this way? If you are not mine, then why does your heart return my call? If you are not mine, would I have the strength to stand at all? I never know what the future brings, but I know you are here with me now, we'll make it through.

And I hope you are the one I share my life with. I don't want to run away, but I can't take it, I don't understand, if I'm not made for you then why does my heart tell me that I am? Is there any way that I can stay in your arms? If I don't need you, then why am I crying on my bed? If I don't need you then why does your name resound in my head? If you're not for me, then why does this distance maim my life? If you're not for me, then why do I dream of you as my wife?

I don't know why you're so far away, but I know that this much is true. We'll make it through, and I hope you are the one I share my life with. I wish that you could be the one I die with, and I pray you're the one I build my home with. I hope I love you all my life. I don't want to run away, but I can't take it. I don't understand, if I'm not made for you then why does my heart tell me that I am? Is there any way that I can stay in your arms?

Because I miss your body and soul so strong that it takes my breath away, and I breathe you into my heart and pray for the strength to stand today. Because I love you, whether it's wrong or right, and though I can't be with you tonight, you know my heart is by your side. I don't want to run away, but I can't take it. I don't understand; if I'm not made for you, why does my heart tell me I am? Is there any way I can stay in your arms?

His creativity made me feel special. I had heard the song by Daniel Bedingfield before, but its meaning took on a greater significance. Realizing the circumstances of our situation and the time apart before seeing each other again, I cried as I read each line. Days after he left, I returned to Fiji for my second year. Over the following year, our relationship continued. He in Australia, me in Fiji; it worked somehow.

When I turned 21, I decided to serve my church by completing a mission. Serving God was the right choice for me, but leaving Tee was not easy. Knowing that he would be waiting for me on the other side of my mission assured and gave me strength. It had always been my dream to marry my best friend, and Tee was that person. I could be myself around him. We helped each other be better people and worked toward our dreams.

After 19 months, I returned home. Minutes after I walked in, Tee called. Though time passed, our feelings for each other did not change. Communicating with him brought butterflies to my stomach. His voice was filled with excitement as he reminded me of our deal. "Remember, that deal we made so long ago?" Of course, I remembered that deal. It was the deal that would define my future. We would get engaged. We made a date for our families to meet and have an engagement ceremony. "It's about time," my aunt yelled as I lunged forward to hang up the phone. My family knew about our long-term relationship. It seemed apparent to everyone but me that we would eventually be each others forever.

A few days later, my cousins unexpectedly showed up. My aunt greeted them and carried on a brief conversation. When they left, my aunt called me. "Grace, I have some devastating news to share with you." My heart began to sink as soon as I saw the tears in her eyes forming.

What is it? I asked. She grabbed my hands and told me Tee had impregnated another woman. Shocked, confused, devastated, and heartbroken, I wondered how could he have failed to mention this when we talked the other night? I was so mad and embarrassed. I just wanted to end it all right then and there.

A Quick Rebound

Not long after our relationship ended, I was accepted into an American University for further studies. It was just what I needed. I'd never been to Hawai'i before, and I was excited about this opportunity, but most of all, I was just excited to leave.

Moving to Hawai'i was great. It seemed like a vacation, as I lived and worked in paradise. Employed at the Polynesian Cultural Center, my first job was selling beverages and snacks at canoe shows. It may not have been the most glamorous, but I enjoyed it. After a few months, I was recruited to dance in the shows. Dancing has been a part of my life ever since I began walking. From the concession cart, dancing on canoes looked easy. I was wrong. The movement of the canoe made even standing difficult, much less dancing.

My first day performing was a beautiful warm day. All my friends came to cheer me on from the stands. I was extremely nervous. I hadn't practiced the routine on a canoe, and it showed. Scared to fall in the water, I looked like a robot. My boss seemed highly disappointed as he watched from a small hut by the pond. I felt so hot, so nervous, so scared - I knew I had let everyone down. It was a nightmare, but at least I didn't fall.

I'd been dating on and off throughout my time at school, but it wasn't anything serious. Jerod and I were friends for a long time. But things started getting serious as graduation neared. After graduation, I would return home to Kiribati, so there was no way I would start a relationship then. He had past issues with long-distance relationships and asked if I could stay in Hawai'i for him. I told him it was impossible, and that's when he asked to move our relationship to the next level. We dated for two weeks before getting engaged, and a week later, we would be married.

It was a typical September day. On my bed, the sun's warmth blanketed my face as cool sea breezes caressed my body. I felt the specialness of the day with each breath; it was my wedding day.

The phone rang. "Hello? I need to talk to you about something."

It was my fiancé's ex-girlfriend. My heart began to race. I wanted to hang up, but I couldn't. The tone of her voice told me something was wrong. I listened. She told me of nights and days she spent with Jerod behind my back.

If true, I thought, I would not marry him. I believed her. Feeling horrible, I called my fiancée's family. I wanted to stop the wedding. They had spent so much money on the ceremony and were good people, and canceling didn't seem fair.

Jerod and two of his brother's wives were in my room within minutes of the phone call. Almost family, we instantly became strangers. Crying, I began; *I don't want to get married anymore.* His brothers' wives were confused.

I turned to Jerod. *This is your chance, to tell the truth; it's not too late. I have already talked to your ex-girlfriend.*

Though admitting to cheating, he still wanted to marry me.

Marriage is not a game, I told him.

At one point, it seemed that both wives were on my side, but they quickly changed opinions when Jerod pleaded.

"See? He still wants to marry you," they said. I was speechless.

"Do you know why I want to marry you," Jerod asked as we made our way to the wedding license office?

Without hesitation, I asked, *why, Jerod?* He said I was the one who could make him a better person. He needed me. I forgave him and married him that afternoon. Together, we overcame disaster, and everything seemed right.

A few days later, when gathering laundry, I noticed something. The computer was on. *Strange, maybe he forgot to turn it off,* I thought. I moved the mouse and saw a message to his ex. In detail, he explained his regret in marrying me. My soul was crushed again. I dropped the laundry and ran out of the room. Was my marriage worth saving? A man's happiness rests in his heart, and clearly, I did not make him happy.

I worried about what others would think of me back home. What gossip would start, and how it could ruin my life. My husband left me for another woman just days after our wedding. Ashamed and embarrassed, I didn't eat. I secluded myself from others. I cried for hours in our bathroom with the shower running so others couldn't hear.

When I pulled myself together, I prayed for healing. During those days, my friends Mary, Julie, Tamika, and Tonie were the ones who comforted me. Their kindness was unforgettable. I would lie down on my bed and stare at the ceiling. I didn't feel the sun's warmth or cool breezes. I didn't want to feel anything. *Why did this happen to me? I was willing to help Jerod become a better man,* but I was the fool in the end. I poured my heart out to the Lord, asking for a sign. I needed help. After praying, I felt nothing. I waited, looking for anything; I saw nothing.

One of my friends suggested a movie to take my mind off everything the following night. Convinced a movie would be a waste of time, I humored her and watched. Halfway through the film, I felt something indescribable. It was as if a heavy weight inside of me lifted. Was this what I was praying for? Yes! Peace! My soul felt restored, and I smiled.

Jerod and I still lived in the same apartment, but he never spent any time there. He returned for daily needs, and I avoided him. I was ashamed. When he returned the following day, things changed. I felt nothing but peace. I started talking to him. He was surprised. I accepted that I could do nothing to change the situation and asked him to sit down for dinner. I told him I didn't want to force him into something he didn't want. It would not be right, and we would have to move forward separately.

That night, both of us agreed to a separation. I packed my bags and prepared to leave the country. I hoped people back home had not heard about my one-week marriage. But the news had spread like wildfire, and everyone seemed to know a different version of the truth. Though rumors flew, I didn't let them ruin me. I knew the truth.

Within one week, I knew what love, betrayal, loss, and ultimately, forgiveness felt like; and it was forgiveness that freed me from everything.

***

After returning to the islands, Jerod's ex-girlfriend applied for a part-time position at my school. Not growing up in Kiribati, adjustment was hard on her. Everything was new. I saw her sitting by herself at a bus stop, and by then, I had long forgiven her.

It was not easy, but I knew forgiveness meant nothing if I couldn't be there for her. We ended all communication after the wedding, but there, as I put myself in her shoes, I felt nothing but empathy for her. My stomach was doing cartwheels as I walked towards her. She warmed up to me immediately, and we were like old friends after the first hello.

Finally, forgiveness.

Finally, peace.

I ignored the red flags

* ★ *

Abuse in any form remains with victims. Whether physical or emotional, abuse impacts can be permanent in victims' lives. Domestic violence is one of the most common forms of abuse worldwide. In Kiribati, females are more commonly abused by males, so it was with me.

***

My cousin was a beautiful woman. She and her husband quickly created a family when they settled down. It was a relationship everyone in the village envied. However, at the age of 23, she passed away. Her husband was heartbroken, and her children did not understand. At that time, I had been married and separated; a new relationship was the last thing on my mind. However, this young man's story attracted me. Maybe since my first marriage did not work out, I could help this young family. *Finally*, I thought, *someone meant for me.*

American Asylee

We lived on different islands during the first few months of our relationship. Communication was through phone and email only. In Kiribati, relationships typically start in the village. There is little to no separation between partners. The relationship we had was very different. It traveled a great distance through technology. To me, the long-distance relationship was romantic.

He was ambitious. His work was his life. He helped communities improve their well-being through agriculture. The more I learned about him, the harder I fell. After one month, we decided to meet in person.

It was night when he arrived. "How can I see you if you remain in the dark," he said, pulling me into the light. I laughed. The person in front of me was much better than anyone I had imagined. He was young, intelligent, good-looking, and funny. He stayed on my island for four days before returning home. I never felt so sure about anything before in my life and could not wait to move forward, or so I thought. After we began a relationship, something changed. He became possessive and began making rules. I was not allowed to go out with my friends. I needed to call and tell him where I was.

By then, I had lived all over the world on my own. The rules he made seemed odd. Without telling him, I decided to go out with friends from high school. I was so excited since it had been years since we had seen each other. When he found out, he was furious. Finding me later that night, he cornered and reprimanded me for breaking his rules. "If you ever do that again," he said, throwing his phone on the ground, "I will do much worse than that to you." Never had I ever felt so scared. His anger was uncontrollable.

Maybe I should end our relationship before it gets worse, I thought. *No, I can't. I am the one who wanted this.* Somehow, having him justified everything I went through in Hawai'i. He was brought into my life to fix what my cousin's death broke. The situation was written in the stars. We were destined for each other. If this relationship were meant to be, as I was sure it was, I had to live with his anger.

He used to take his anger out on things. One time he hit the side of the bed so hard while I was on it, I thought it was going to break. Another time he threw my journal out the car window while driving — he knew how much it meant to me. Never did he lay a hand on me then. Because of this, I felt safe. After we married, he began taking his anger out on me.

***

I've had chronic back pain since I fell out of a tree when nine years old. I've learned to live with it, but the pain is too much some days. We were returning from my aunt's house, where I went for back treatments when the abuse began.

Filled with potholes from the week's rain, the road was unbearable. "Why don't both of you remain here," my aunt asked. "Just for three days until your back is healed. The road is horrible."

I told her we would think about it, but my husband decided that we needed to return home. Bumping, jerking, and bouncing, the one-hour trip took us two. Finally, frustrated and in pain, I told him *it would have been better if I had stayed!* That's when he exploded.

He started calling me names, accusing me of being a bad person and wanting to leave. People watched as he hit everything around him, including me. The first punch put me on the floor. Not knowing what to do, I cried and apologized. *I won't go! I won't go!*

He scolded me. I was embarrassed for myself and my family. Everyone knew that he was abusive, and soon after, more rules were added. I was not to attend school events without consent. I was not to interact with the opposite sex, and I had to go to his island whenever summoned. This demoralized me.

It would have been bearable once a month, but each week was like an indentured servitude I paid for my first broken marriage. Weekends became my most hectic days between packing, preparing lessons, and leaving work early to board the last canoe.

Hours spent on the open sea to honor his rules shredded my self-respect. After a day with him, I would jump on the first canoe back to my island and resume life.

It would have been different if I did this out of love, but it wasn't. It was out of fear. I never wanted this. *How did I get here? Why did I get here?* I kept a smile on my face to hide everything underneath, hoping people would assume I was just young and in love. Which, at one point, I was. But now, no. My life was caged above the open ocean. It was not right, and I knew it. It was not healthy, and I was anything but safe. I lost count of times I feared death at his hands. Bruises heal, but fear didn't.

Out of desperation, I began abusing myself. Something inside me forced me to beat myself whenever he exploded in anger. Beating myself stopped him from beating me. The first time I hit myself was in our car. At that point, the abuse had been normalized in our relationship. I hated it.

I began by banging my head against the window. I did this until I was dizzy. He watched. If anyone were to hit me, it would be me from then on. I took away his power and restored mine. It was liberating. I caused my pain, not him.

I experimented with gasoline. I picked up the container as if to throw it down and set everything on fire.

But, instead, I brought it to my lips and began drinking. It burned.

The chemicals destroyed my stomach. Bubbles formed. It was as if I was hungry, but I wasn't. Each gulp more bubbles and they hurt. *Breathe*, I would tell myself, *just breathe*. When his temper cooled, I thought about what I had done. I wouldn't tell him about my stomach or the oily residue in my mouth. I was broken. My life was worthless, and there was no way out. Creative acts of torture just created a better show, but all I wanted was to end his abuse. Ultimately, it didn't matter. No matter what, I ended up bruised, poisoned, and beaten for a past I could not fix.

In Kiribati, women are prized for their virginity. I was not a virgin, and he knew this. He assured me I had nothing to worry about since he, too, had a past. I reminded him that we both had pasts we could do nothing about. This angered him even more. It reminded him that his wife, my cousin, was gone. "My past is different," he'd say. "She is no longer alive." At the mention of her name, he became abusive, leaving me in pain and filled with fear. We both needed more time to heal from our pasts before settling down, but he insisted on moving forward, and I was too scared to say no. My first marriage didn't work out, and I was determined not to have another broken marriage. But eventually, I had had enough.

I decided to confront him. He needed to let me go. This would solve all our problems. I would be honest, sincere, patient, calm, and straightforward. Surely, he would listen to reason, and hopefully, he would understand. We couldn't stay this way. His children, our anger, and my body were all suffering.

Ready to present my case, I proposed a talk. He decided we should leave the house and went to a nearby bridge on his motorcycle. I asked for a divorce and to return to my family. Deep down, I knew this was not a good idea, but I was desperate. Returning would be the quickest way to stop the violence. Stopping me, he said he had heard enough, and we needed to return. Confused, I obliged. I didn't want to upset him further. My confusion turned to worry when I realized we were not going home. We ended up in the back of his office, where he beat me. I covered my head to avoid the blunt object in his hand. I gasped for air when it hit my back. Seconds later, another hit. No longer protecting my face, my arms went to my back. Another strike. This one on my arms. I cried for mercy, a halt, anything to stop the beating. Mutilating myself was not an option. He was in control.

"Do you want to leave me now? I will take you to the small pond and drown you before I let you leave me!" If I looked at him, he would have killed me. I laid lifeless on the ground. *Was this how my life would end? Would I die here?* I thought. My legs were bruised and red with blood. My hand brushed against a stone. This was my only chance. I crawled towards it, lifted it, and picked it up to hit my head. Lunging, he grabbed the stone from my hands. His demeanor changed. His voice lowered. "I will kill you if you ever think about leaving me again. It would be better if you die alone than seeing you with another man."

He intimated, manipulated, and instilled fear in me. I dreaded leaving him because I feared him. I lived with the abuse for two years and blamed myself for everything. Aware of my past and imperfections, he was the only one who would take me in. I owed everything to him. Trapped, beatings became routine, and arguments were daily.

After dancing in a village celebration, he took me to another secluded location a month later. Again, he was angry with me. A flower had fallen from my hair, and a friend of his placed it behind my ear. He hit me for allowing another man to put a flower in my hair. I screamed. He grabbed my face and squeezed my mouth until I stopped yelling. I couldn't open my mouth. The pain was unbearable. I remained silent the rest of the day. Again, I thought, *how could I let myself get here?* Later, he apologized and promised to change. He asked for forgiveness. Out of fear, I forgave him and hoped for a better tomorrow.

By this time, I was two months pregnant. I thought things would change. I loved children. Having one inside of me was surreal. I thought about my baby every time I caressed my growing stomach. Forgetting my past, I was happy. I wondered what they would look like. Who would they become? I thought about my husband's sons and how they would react if it were a girl. They had always wanted a sister.

At first, he was excited. But soon began questioning how I would treat his children if I had one of my own? How could he ask this? Did he not realize that the child was also his? During my third month, the aggression returned.

We were in our room when he twisted my arms around my back. His mother heard my cries and yelled from outside, "What's going on?"

"Nothing," he yelled back, "We are just playing." Silently, I cried.

Later that day, we went to my cousin's house. Both of us were invited in, but he refused and decided to stay in the car. When I returned, he was drenched in sweat. The heat of the vehicle matched his anger. Berating me as we drove away, he hit my head. Shocked that he continued to beat me while pregnant, I cried. He stopped the car and ordered me to drive. I said nothing and moved to the driver's seat. Sitting behind me, he began kicking my chair.

Our seats were not secured, and I lunged forward, hitting the steering wheel with my chest. Pain radiated from my back. I was furious and began pounding my stomach. It was the only thing that made him stop. My child did not deserve us, an abusive father, and a mother too scared to leave.

I lost my child that day.

The miscarriage began at night. Twisting in agony, I laid in the hospital staring at the green walls. I felt as if I were going to die again. Breathing was hard, and blood was everywhere. Each step to the restroom was like a step closer to death. At first, the blackouts felt good. They were a welcomed escape, but eventually, I lost energy. Breathing became too great of a challenge.

Enough is Enough, I told myself. *If I walk out of this alive, I will never go back.* After too many years of being a victim, I had to leave. The day I lost my child was the day everything changed. Years of abuse nearly killed me. If I didn't do anything to save myself, no one would.

As determined as I was to improve my situation, the abuse continued. After my miscarriage, I took some time off before returning to work. Traveling to his island on the weekends also resumed at this time.

Several months later, my mother and sister decided to visit us for the weekend. It was the first and only time they did. Per Kiribati tradition, I left my family to live with him when our relationship became official. So having my family with us for the weekend meant the world to me.

On the weekend of the visit, my mother and sister traveled by boat; I followed the following day by plane. My husband was excited to see me until I told him that my family was also coming for the weekend.

"Is that what you think about? Your family, not me?" he said. *I didn't mean any offense,* I explained. *It's just that it's their first time to spend a weekend with us; I thought you would be happy.* I could tell that he was furious, and once we arrived home, it got even worse. My mother pulled me aside to tell me of a woman selling dried pandanus leaves in the village. She loved weaving mats but getting leaves on her island was difficult. I told her that I would purchase the leaves for her without hesitation.

I thought my husband wouldn't mind if I bought them, but I was wrong. Smoldering, he asked to have another conversation with me in private. I followed him to an isolated guest house where he began yelling at me, and before I knew it, he started strangling me with a small towel. "Just because you earn money, it doesn't mean it is yours to give away." His hands tightened the towel as he scolded me. Gasping for air through my mouth and nose, I did everything I could to stop him, but he was too strong.

Eventually, he decided to let me go. I didn't say anything. However, once I was able to breathe, I screamed for help. Like a switch, his demeanor changed. He apologized and assured me that he meant no harm. I continued crying. Finally, his behavior reverted again, and he said, "before, when I hit you, I felt bad afterward, but this time I'm not." That passive-aggressive apology was all I needed to confirm my need to act.

***

Growing up, I witnessed my father beat my mother. My siblings and I would run away when he got into one of his moods. We would wait outside and keep watch at night, waiting for the lights to turn off. That was our signal. When the lights went out, we knew our father had fallen asleep. We would tiptoe back inside to fall asleep again. Like me, my mother would cry for mercy when no longer able to bear the pain. She wore sunglasses to work the following day to hide the bruises. The more I thought about my mother, the more I realized I would end up just like her if I did not leave.

She didn't want us to grow up without a father. Her love for us was stronger than my father's fist. The loss of my child gave me courage. Filled with regret, my child gave me the courage to leave.

My mother reminded me of the countless other women who experienced the same thing in the hospital. *Think about those women;* she would say, *who've been abused and have remained with their husbands. They think there's no way out! Maybe you could show them that there's a way if you leave.* She saw me as hope for all abused women in Kiribati.

It's not about breaking a relationship, she said. *It's about showing our men what is right. They won't know until we stand up. No woman deserves abuse, fear, or death. No woman.*

After two years, I was finally ready to take a stand. Convinced it would be easier to leave in secrecy, I waited for my husband to go on an international business trip before running away.

On a leap of faith

I converted to the Church of Jesus Christ of Latter-day Saints when I was 18 years old. Never had I been so moved by religion. I immediately wanted to share it with everyone. The church had a global youth missionaries' program, and I wanted to go immediately; however, as a female, I needed to wait until I was 21. I prepared for a mission by becoming more involved with the church during those years. In school, I competed for a limited number of overseas university scholarships. My family counted on me to do my best, so I studied during the day and attended missionary prep courses in the evenings. I worked hard and had faith that God would reward me for my efforts. At the end of my senior year, I received a scholarship to Fiji's University of the South Pacific.

January 2006

I was amazed at the beautiful sights approaching mountainous islands that jumped out of the ocean. It was the first time I saw mountains. Kiribati was all I knew until then, and it was extremely small. *Fiji is way too big for me,* I thought. Everything was new and exciting, except for one thing, English. In high school, I loathed English. I struggled to complete assignments and did not feel the slightest bit of confidence in my abilities. In Fiji, English was everywhere: on signs, books, and TV. At university, I avoided the constant barrage of English by sticking with other Kiribati students. I lived, worked, and partied with them. The one place I couldn't escape English was at church.

I joined a small church not far from campus. I was the only Kiribati person in the congregation. I was trapped; I had to speak English. Scared others would hear my broken English; I darted home immediately after the final prayer. A silent escape was my preferred tactic. Conversing in English was hard. My thoughts were in Kiribati, which made speaking in Kiribati easy. I couldn't think in English. I had to translate my thoughts before speaking, which took time. No one enjoys conversations punctuated with pregnant pauses.

After two months, the bishop asked me for a one-on-one meeting. *Was he upset with me for always running away after the service? Was I in trouble?* Greeting me as I approached the church, he took me into his office and presented me with an opportunity. "I want you to be the ward's new single adult president." I laughed and replied, *why me? There are plenty of single adults who speak English here, and I can barely communicate.*

"Grace," he responded, "You are precisely the right person for this calling. God uses our imperfections to show others his power through overcoming the impossible." He was right. I had no choice. I was the one who needed the most help with English. I had to show others the power of God through me. I accepted the calling.

On my way back to the apartment, I began worrying. No one in the group spoke my language. *How in the world would I do this? What if they don't understand me? What if I'm not the leader they want? How will I communicate?* I tried to call my bishop and tell him I had changed my mind, but my conscience got the best of me. I promised myself never to turn down a calling. I couldn't let myself down. I had to make this work.

I made a script for my first meeting. For days, I practiced my delivery. The hours of each day moved fast. Too fast. I wished for more time, but Sunday came, and before I knew it, I was standing in front of a large group of single adults.

Before beginning, I silently prayed for help. My heart raced as I began talking. Voice quivering, all eyes on me, petrified; I forgot every word I prepared. I felt foolish. I was not ready. To my surprise, people began participating. "Keep going. You're doing fine!" They encouraged me and made me feel safe. I started remembering all I had practiced at home and finished my first meeting with nothing but smiles from the audience.

After a few months, my challenges seemed small and distant. I grew into my role and began enjoying every Sunday. I stopped running away at the end of service. I accepted my weaknesses and turned to God for guidance. Through others, he helped me. Mary, from Niue, and Mabu from Tuvalu made it their mission to help me with English, and after two years, speaking English was second nature. Church life was beautiful, classes were great, and I was nearing my 21st birthday. Serving a mission would take me away from home. I was torn between God and my family.

The day after my 21st birthday, I went to church services seeking guidance. Sister Moli oversaw Sunday school that day. Halfway through class, she looked at me and said, "If you want to do something that you know is right, do it." I knew God was using her to guide me as soon as she said that. Suddenly, schooling was no longer important to me. I recommitted myself to mission prep courses and informed my family of my decision.

My state president called to inform my bishop of my mission. In his office, my hands shook while receiving the envelope. I could not open it. I handed the envelope to my friend Macy. "Grace, she said, you have been called to serve in the Philippines!" Overwhelmed, my mind raced. New languages, cultures, and people waiting for me in the Philippines? I couldn't stop shaking with excitement. It was then, halfway through my studies, I quit and went to serve my mission in the Philippines.

Come what may, and love it

──────── ★ ★ ★ ────────

In his last general conference speech, Elder Joseph B. Wirthlin reflected on the ups and downs of life. "Come what may and love it," he said. He challenged us to love no matter what. "The next time you're tempted to groan, try to laugh; it will extend your life and make the lives of those around you happier." Preparations for my mission were filled with inspirational lessons like this.

Early in my mission, my companion and I hopped into a jitney. We were headed to the next town when both of us noticed a strong smell coming from the pig in the back seat. Before complaining about the smell, I laughed. I tried to make light of the situation as we bounced down the road. The driver drove as if nothing was wrong and wondered why we were laughing. He must have been driving with that pig for so long that he became desensitized to its smell. When we returned home, I shared Elder Wirthlin's message with my companion, *come what may, and love it*.

I believe prayer creates bridges between Heavenly Father and us by filling our hearts with God's love. It's simple to pray but praying is not enough. We must know how to receive responses to our prayers. Acting on prayer shows how much we recognize and appreciate God's responses. Some prayers will go unanswered, but we must trust God knows what's best for us.

December 24, 2008

It was my first Christmas away from home. Our mission president allowed each of us to call home, something most of us were excited about. However, I declined the opportunity and decided to do Christmas caroling that night with my companion. We prayed for guidance before leaving our apartment, hoping to find someone in need of company that night. *How about the Pablo family,* I asked? Though the family lived far from us, my companion had no problem with it.

However, since it was Christmas, all public transport had been canceled. My companion worried about traveling so far on Christmas and suggested a family closer to us. Something inside me did not want to go. I pleaded for the Pablo family, and she agreed. We continued to wait on the side of the road, and within 15 minutes, a jeepney came! Worried that he might not make it home in time for celebrations, the driver pulled over after about 20 minutes and said, "I am sorry, but I cannot take you any further." We were far from our destination and had to walk the rest of the way. The sun was setting, and many people were already drunk. Darkness was quickly approaching. Asking for protection, I prayed as we walked. "Sister James! Sister Matiban!" It was our mission President. He was on his way to pick up his kids from the town we were heading to. It was a sign; the Pablo family needed us. Jumping in his car, we were in front of their house in less than ten minutes!

The house was dark and quiet. All other places were loud and filled with people. "Maybe they went somewhere else to celebrate Christmas," my companion said.

My heart sank. *We couldn't have traveled all this way for anything. There were too many signs leading us here.* I walked up to the house, calling their names, but received no response. I waited in the patch of dirt right in front of their window until I heard something. I saw movement. Then one of their children came out. In the sweetest voice, she asked, "Why are you here?"

We want to sing Christmas carols with you if that's okay. But if not, that's okay too, we understand. She went back inside, and seconds later, the father opened the door. He said, "We don't mind at all. Please come in!" Taken into their house, we sat and began singing Christmas carols. It turned into the most beautiful night.

Whenever we visited them, the mother would distance herself from us. It seemed we were a bother to her. When the carols ended, I asked if anyone wanted to say anything. Surprisingly, she raised her hand. I was worried. Did we upset her? Her eyes filled with tears as she began to speak.

Before you came, I forced my kids to go to sleep. Both my husband and I don't work. I did not want our children to see what was happening outside. Our neighbors celebrated with gifts and special foods that we could not afford. So it was better if my children fell asleep and did not see Christmas. But, while I was putting them to sleep, I prayed for the first time. I asked God why they had to suffer?

Then both of you showed up, and we celebrated Christmas. The Lord heard my prayer and brought both of you here to let us know we were not forgotten. Singing songs, sharing good messages, and enjoying our time together as a family; was more than I prayed for. I know the Lord genuinely loves my family. He brought you to us. Thank you.

That Christmas was the most beautiful one I ever experienced. We prayed for a task, saw God's plan, heard the calling, and did the work. The Lord is always mindful of us and loves us, no matter how poor or lonely we think we are. We always matter to him, and he is always there for us. That night I was reminded of Sister Moli's message, "if you want to do something you know is right, do it." God works through us, but only if we have faith to act on what we pray for. We can all be the answer to someone's prayer.

***

After returning from my mission, I connected with an American family who served a mission in my home ward. They would eventually call me their Kiribati daughter, and I would call them my American parents. Keeping in touch, we called and wrote to each other regularly. I turned to them for help when seeking to escape an abusive relationship.

Though safe, on a visitor's visa, I knew eventually I would have to return. I spent months thinking of ways to stay in the U.S. legally. I applied to jobs here and there, hoping to obtain a work visa. Most times, I felt like I was wasting my time. It was horrible. I needed to move forward with something. I wished my American parents could have adopted me, but it was impossible.

After two months, an aunt in England contacted me. She wanted me to perform at her grandson's first birthday party. "Since you are in America now, your ticket will be cheap. I will pay for your trip, but it won't be free. You will need to dance for your ticket."

My entire family knew I loved dancing, and this was the break I needed. It's what I had been praying for. England was my answer. I finally saw the light at the end of the tunnel; I had to make sure my performance was worth my ticket. I practiced a lot. Although it was hard at first, it all came back to me since I hadn't danced in a while.

Quickly, the day came, and I was heading to England. The flight attendants were making their final cabin checks when I overheard someone say, "I can't believe it will take 11 hours to get there. It's going to be a very long ride." I chuckled, remembering all my previous international flights. I fell asleep minutes after takeoff, and when I woke, I was landing at Heathrow airport.

After immigration, I was taken to my aunt's house, where I met relatives I had never met before. Everything felt like home—but we were in England. For a month, I stayed with my family, enjoying the sights and sounds of London.

American Asylee

When I returned to the United States, my re-entry was smooth. The only immigration question posed to me was if I had been to the USA before. I answered affirmatively, and my passport was stamped. Like that, my visa was extended for another six months. *I thought this might be how I could legally stay in the United States.* Immediately, I started making plans for my next trip: this time, Australia.

Dear diary

— ★ ★ ★ —

Four months after I returned, I decided to celebrate Kiribati independence with my aunt in Australia. Leaving the United States mid-summer for Australia's winter was a huge shock. It had been years since I saw my aunt, and when I arrived, she was extremely busy. Immediately thrown on her prep crew, I went shopping for the ceremony. It brought back so many memories of Kiribati. The rice, the fish, the flowers, and the Australian currency. It was just like home, but bigger. "You know Grace," my aunt said, "I am so glad you are here to celebrate with us! Being so far from home, this is a special time for all of us." I was so happy to celebrate Kiribati independence in Australia that year.

Excited to meet other I-Kiribati, I began noticing people avoiding me. I didn't mind until the alcohol revealed why. Drunk, they approached and asked me why I left my husband. In Kiribati, leaving one's husband is taboo. I tried explaining my circumstances, but my words fell on deaf ears. Rumors from Kiribati dominated their minds. I was a bad person. I tried to ignore them but knew no matter how hard I tried, it didn't matter. What was supposed to be a celebratory escape turned out to be a horrible nightmare. I left the ceremony feeling worse than when I arrived. *Would I be able to stop the rumors? Would I be able to correct the lies? Or would gossip ruin my reputation?*

Two days before leaving Australia, I received a message from one of my good friends, who expressed his concern. His kindness was comforting, but I did not want another relationship. I was better off alone. As we began talking, I expected him to back off; but he saw things very differently. "This is not your fault," he said.

As much as it pained me to hear him say that, I needed to hear those words. It had been a while since I started thinking positively about myself. He was sincere, family-oriented, and always looking to help others. He seemed to know just what I wanted to hear. The honest conversation exposed our vulnerabilities to each other and made him more than a friend to me that night. His actions proved that I could trust him, regardless of what I thought about men.

He was seven years younger than I, his maturity and intelligence surpassed his age, and despite my past, he loved me for who I was. He found something I thought I had lost and planted a seed of hope in my heart. On my last night in Australia, he asked me to talk with him again. But, since I shared a room with my niece, we ended up texting all night long. I found myself falling for him.

"Everything is worth a try," he said, and I agreed. He invited me over, but my plane was departing in six hours, and I didn't have the money to change plans. My month was over, and I was off to America.

From first-class to jail

★ ★ ★

27 July 2016

It was a chilly morning in Sydney. Not cold, but cool. To many islanders, it would have been freezing, but I'd been in colder places and could appreciate the coolness of the air. The crisp morning and imminent farewells made the car ride seem longer than usual. Each stoplight, each turn, only served to heighten the emotions of all I had gone through over the past few years.

The ticket agent at the counter noticed the buddy pass I was flying on. "It looks like we have one extra premium class seat," she said as she handed the boarding pass to me. I glanced down and read GRACE JAMES: PREM, SEAT 12A. I had never flown premium before, and though excited, I was sad. I didn't want to leave, especially after meeting someone who supported me so much. I had been through a lot and was running anywhere but home for as long as I could. I was running from fear, pain, sorrow, and I felt lost.

Holding the premium class ticket between my fingers as if it were a million dollars, I felt like something big was about to happen. Chills of excitement and sorrow rushed through my veins. I walked towards the security gate, and with only a backpack and sweater, I cleared security in no time. I arrived at my gate nearly two hours ahead of the departure time. I waited and fell asleep.

Attention ladies and gentlemen, we will commence our boarding for flight DL40 bound for Los Angeles in just a few minutes. We ask that you present both your ticket and passport for inspection at the boarding ramp's entrance in preparation for an on-time departure.

The voice over the PA system woke me just in time to take my place in the queue. Directed to the front of the plane, a flight attendant asked if I had any items to store. Shaking my head, no, she continued, "Would you want a beverage or snack?" I smiled and declined.

Awed by all that surrounded me, the size of the pods, the conspicuously hidden collapsible tables, the entertainment screens, and the legroom, I was so grateful for the buddy pass. The kindest flight crew waited on hand and foot the following fourteen hours.

Special premium class menus were distributed throughout the cabin. There were so many foods I had never seen before. I tried them all and fell asleep in my comfy pod as soon as I finished.

I woke during the serving of the second meal. *So, this is what premium class feels like;* I thought as more food lined my tray. Within two hours, we arrived at Los Angeles International Airport, and before long, I again was awaiting re-entry into the United States. In the queue, people of all backgrounds passed through the checkpoint, one by one. Finally, it was my turn.

Officer: *Passport, customs, and arrival documents.*

I handed her my documents.

Officer: Are you transiting?

Not sure what she was asking, I asked if she could repeat herself.

Officer: Are you transiting? Are you going on another international flight?

No, I said.

Officer: Can I see your return ticket?

After she typed in my information, she called her supervisor. Another officer asked me to stand aside. "We will need to bring you into a room for further questioning." I followed him, and in minutes, I faced immediate deportation.

In a state of shock, I asked my officer if it was okay to call my friend. He led me to a room, and I prayed before making the call. Prayer had always been something that guided my life, but it had become something I took for granted during that time. Now, here I was, with no one to call for help. I felt unworthy as if I deserved nothing.

Hoping against hope, I prayed. When finished, I felt a rush of peace fall over me. It had been forever since I felt something like this. Somehow, I knew everything would be okay. I dialed my friend, explained my situation, and within minutes, my ticket was fixed.

The officer entered the room. "Ms. James, get ready for your flight. I will return when it is time to board." I thought, *how can I be at peace in this situation? It was the opposite of what I asked for in my prayer.* Some time passed, and the officer's demeanor changed when he returned. Fiji Airways couldn't return me that night. He had to find an alternative flight, and this would take time. Handcuffed and escorted to another facility, I felt like a criminal. I was ashamed, nervous, and being deported.

As I walked into the facility, a poster entitled "Notice of Advisal" caught my eye. It explained how I had a right to explain my situation back home and seek asylum due to a justified fear. God heard my prayer. I thanked him for his answer, especially since I felt least deserving of his help.

I sat in the holding cell, thinking about what I had lived through for years. I thought about my friends and family waiting to pick me up at the airport. I thought about my family in Kiribati. I was scared, and time stood still.

After a few hours, another officer entered the room. I decided to open up and tell the officer about the beatings, gasoline, my lost child, and my fear of returning home.

"Why didn't you tell me this earlier?" he said. *I didn't know about asylum.* He paused, then said, "If that's the case, you should know that you'll be waiting for a hearing at the detention center. I don't know how long the wait will be. It could be months or even years." He paused for what felt like forever, then asked, "Do you want to stay?" *What is a detention center?* "Jail," he said.

Jail seemed to be the only way to live. Jail was my only hope. *Please, I want to stay and wait for my court date.* With that, he canceled my flight and escorted me back to the holding facility. From there, I was transferred to the detention center, where I would remain for the next thirteen months. It was the scariest decision I ever made, but also the opportunity I prayed for.

A new beginning

It's been nothing but cold. I don't feel my hands anymore as I waited for my officer to tell me when am I going to transfer & where to? As I waited I decided to call my friends/cousins using the phone card my officer gave me. Gladly I was able to talk to John. He sound so worried so I told him that he's got nothing to worry about & that I'm okay. I'm just gonna spend some time in jail & if my case is good then I might come out sooner. He said "How can you sound so calm? You're going to jail and you're okay with it? So I told him " well at least I'm not deported plus I'm not going to be there too.

But this is how it really happened I was praying for the miracle that somehow I won't be deported at that time. I knew that my officer's ans- wer was final but at the same time I still have Hope.

It was when I finished saying my prayer that I felt peace & that everything will be okay but I thought to myself "how is this possible since my ticket is final & even my officer told me that I'm going on a flight that night. At that point I was confuse & doubt the answer that I felt that I'm not goin' to be deported bause I saw my officer getting all things ready for my flight. until later on He came back and was angry telling me that the airline I was going to be on changed their mind in taking me. He said this is impossible, they told me earlier that they can take you & now they can't?" From there, I knew that what I felt was real. You see? God works in mysterious & wonders not according to the way we think or even the logic.

Anyways after many hours in a very cold room finally they decided to transfer me to another cold but this time Its a real cell by myself. The officer there were so cruel but I can understand that its part of their job. Finally around 5-6pm I arrived at JMF.

29th July, 2016
Friday

Unbounded

Precious moments in jail. You might wonder how these two words, *precious* and *moments*, could relate in a jail. For many people, this may sound crazy, but for others, it makes sense. When people hear the word jail, most think nothing but negative thoughts. Separated from loved ones, unable to work, and incarcerated, your freedom is gone, but under the surface, goodness abounds.

My experience in jail was one of the most humbling, challenging, and rewarding experiences of my life. Deciding to see jail as an opportunity changed how I thought, felt, and acted. Fighting for asylum is life-changing. Though I longed for friends and family every day, I didn't need them to experience joy. I didn't have to eat in fancy restaurants or dress in cute clothes; I just needed an attitude of gratitude. With this, anything was possible.

***

American Asylee

One of the first people I met in jail was Verna Williams. Short, with long black hair, her bright green detainee uniform brightened her tired brown eyes. Her light brown skin and round face reminded me of faces back home. On my first day, she handed me a handmade book and said, "Maybe you could use it as a journal to keep track of everything that happens here." I thanked her for the book and intended to do just as she said. Reflecting on each day, I created my gratitude journal. It helped me keep perspective and how I saw God in jail. It blurred the fact that I was cut off from everything I knew and allowed me to embrace this shared reality with other asylum seekers.

I ended each day recounting the goodness I experienced. It showed me how God's love was greater than any trial we faced. Writing set my mind at ease and made me grateful for all I had. It required a lot of discipline, and some days, I felt I had absolutely nothing to be grateful for. Other days, I was too tired to think about writing. I wavered between nights with nothing to write and nights where I couldn't stop writing. I wanted to share my experiences so readers could understand what asylum seekers go through one day. This is what kept me going.

No matter how tired I was or how long my days were, the thought of people eventually reading my story inspired me. English, not being my first language, I found it difficult to express my feelings. I could not paint elaborate scenes with beautiful words. I didn't care. I didn't give up because I am an immigrant, and we don't know how to give up.

Faith pulled me through many dark and lonely moments in that cold detention center. In detainment, darkness, and loneliness consumed souls. Each night, women older than I cried. Each bunk contained so much pain. This new place was scary.

My gratitude journal helped me focus on things that gave me joy and hope. It helped me appreciate what little I had and made me realize that there was always something to be grateful for regardless of my situation. I was blessed with another day, another meal, another moment, and gratitude was how I began each entry. Recording gratitude changed reality and prepared me for bigger things, challenges, and gifts. Others in the facility saw my journal as a lengthy letter to my Australian "what if." Though true, its ultimate purpose was hope in a hopeless situation.

My Free

30th JULY, 2016
Saturday

"Friendship ISN'T about who you've KNOWN the Longest. It's about who walked Into your Life said "I'm Here 4 you" & proved it"

I'm just grateful for my new & great funny friends Crys & Martha they made laugh so much during our lunch that we had outside the yard. Being around positive & people who just embrace the present for what it is is just amazing & I'm just so happy. Not to forget my best friend Priscilla for reminding me about rules so that I won't get in trouble

Mahal Kita

Call

Everytime a new detainee arrived, they get to have a free call to do only within the store of course so since I wasn't able to make one yesterday thank goodness they let me today. I get to talk to uncle & told him what's going on. One of my good friends also told me that I need not to worry about anything. This is the great blessing to have people who are willing to stand by your side esp in your hardest time.

Also my neighbor/my best friend/more like my mother verna came over to me with a pouch. She made it from her brown paper & not just that but she even put some commissary food inside which I'm so thankful for cause I know its very hard to have food in this place. It's been such a great day, my first full day here in jail

Changes

★ ★ ★

On my first day, I was assigned mop duty. I had to clean the entire day room. I'd never used a mop before because we never had a floor in Kiribati. Each time I saw my name on the list, I imagined each chore's difficulty and counted the hours before the next assignment. I never wanted to clean. Some days other detainees had to wake me up to clean.

If I continued like this, there's no way I would enjoy my time in jail. If I wanted to make this experience as great as possible, I had to change. In my second month, we moved to a new room. On the first morning in our new location, I asked the person responsible for assignments to give me the names of those assigned mopping detail for the week. Since mopping was the most challenging task, and our new room was much larger, I wanted the job for the entire week. Approaching each assigned person, I asked for permission to take over their assignment. At first, they laughed. They knew I hated mopping, but they were happy when they realized I was serious.

On the first day, I almost gave up. Halfway through, I ran out of breath. The following days were still challenging but more manageable. I began to enjoy it. I recorded the names of women who allowed me to complete their chores in my journal. Some were older women who had trouble bending down to pick up pieces of paper. I had a young body, but it was soft. Jail chores hardened me. I couldn't believe the enjoyment I found in mopping. My mother would have been shocked to have a daughter who cleaned.

I continued doing this until others started complaining about the assignments they didn't have. So, I found other ways of keeping busy. I would scrub, tidy, and wash anything I could to stay active. When people tried to stop me, others in the room would say, "Don't bother, she likes to work," or "That's just how she is." As the months passed, I began to think to myself; *I can't believe I did it, I've changed!* I was known for my laziness at home, but I was anything but in jail.

The officers saw my work ethic and eventually recommended me for a "house mouse" position. I was in charge of creating cleaning schedules, helping new detainees assimilate, preparing equipment, and watching after fellow detainees. It was my first position in jail, and I enjoyed it. Without changing my old ways, I wouldn't have had the opportunity. It felt so good to be needed, respected, and accountable. In jail, I learned how to help others; and by helping others, I was helped. Sometimes, we believe our weaknesses are impossible to change. But it's not until we first change our attitude that we discover we can.

MY Cleaning SERVICE

Date	Name of person & #	Date	Name & Name#	Date	Name & #
11/10/16	Martha Nfoneh # 11	11/13/16	Page Sweep		
11/11/16	Eneyda Molina # 10		Maria C. Urrutia #36		
11/12/16	Aracely Meza # 34				
11/14/16	Sunday myself				
11/15/16	Eneyda Molina # 10				
11/16/	Toorunda Reyrona #21				
11/17/16	Emma Muniz # 33				
11/18/16	sweep Patricia Nevares # 42				
11/19/16	for myself Sunday				
11/20/16	mop Claudia Bechelo # 82				
11/21/16	Aracely meza # 34				
11/23/16	Glenda Martinez # 50				
11/24/16	Heavy period day # day for				
11/28/16	heavy sweep for Patricia Nevares # 42				
11/29/16	myself				
12/12/16	mop & sweep restroom Aracely Meza # 34				
12/3/16	mop & sweep restroom mrs Gabriel #44				
12/3/16	mopping the room maria Eugenia # 38				
12/5/16	Sunday myself				
12/6/16	cleaning equipment Preparation				
12/8/16	mop & sweep maritza Nevares # 52				
12/9/16	patricia sweep Venus Swiss # 34				
12/11/16	sweep bathroom Judith # 52				
12/11/16	Sunday errand				
12/11/16	Nasreen, toronto &				
Reagan	visit Dr Patricia C.				

Church Days

Leaving the facility was always a treat. It didn't matter where we were going. What mattered was that we were getting out. Staying in one place for too long can be devastating. I looked forward to our Tuesday church days. It was our day to focus on God, the giver of hope, love, and strength.

"Church time, church time," the deputy would call as everyone gathered with Bibles in hand. English and Spanish services were provided. The Spanish services always had more participants. Chinese detainees often went with the English group, which typically had only 4 or 5. Those who stayed behind usually spent time playing cards, sleeping, or watching movies. As we moved to the exit, deputies frisked us to make sure nothing but bibles were with us. Once checked, we walked to our assigned area.

Maggie sat quietly next to a stack of bibles, hoping for new attendees. It saddened me to know most in the group had never owned a Bible before. She always smiled when she saw us. Our weekly assignment was to invite more women to the group so they, too, could hear the good news. Sometimes we succeeded, but most of the time, we didn't. Most didn't speak English.

We would begin with a prayer and then start singing. Maggie knew how much we loved singing, and she was always excited to hear the new songs we practiced throughout the week. Priscilla, one of my African friends, loved singing gospel songs and teaching them to us during our open yard fellowship time. Unless it was a day we were punished, we always had time outside. After singing, Maggie shared God's word. These were the only words that reaffirmed our belief that we were free, no matter what. God's word made us feel that there was hope, and when she finished, she would turn the discussion over to share what we had learned or experienced throughout the week.

Sharing always brought us to tears. Sometimes tears of joy, but most of the time, tears of fear. Maggie always reminded us that fear was the enemy of faith. When we showed fear, we showed weakness in faith. Fear was disbelieving that God would take care of us or that God would forsake us, especially in difficult times. Sometimes, we needed her voice to reassure us of God's love. We needed someone to reassure us that it was okay to be afraid if the fear didn't control our faith, and Maggie was that person.

According to her, fear was the absence of faith. It was easy to let fear win, but our faith needed to be stronger than fear. Faith helped us fend off sadness and loneliness. Faith gave us hope that things would get better. Faith assured us that our present situation wouldn't last forever, and we would be reunited with loved ones again. Faith was the force that enabled us to move forward, knowing that positive things would happen one day.

Maggie loved testimonies and would always ask us to share how God helped us and how we saw him during these times. Sharing testimonies was my favorite part of the service. The personal testimonies were challenging, but we shared. As a result, we felt closer to each other and realized how much we needed each other to move forward.

Testimonies usually had these words scattered throughout them. "I'm grateful to become part of this group because it helps me to know more about God's word." Church time always flew. Deputies often raised their hands before everyone shared, and it was time for us to say our thank yous and goodbyes for the week.

We always lined up to re-enter the jail by the flowers. The facility we lived in was on a farm with many flowers. My favorite flower, the plumeria, grew near the jail. Blooming continuously in ideal conditions reminded me of home and the people I loved. It reminded me of dancing, laughing, and all the things I enjoyed doing on the outside. Its constant presence told me that goodness still existed in my life, and one day, I would return.

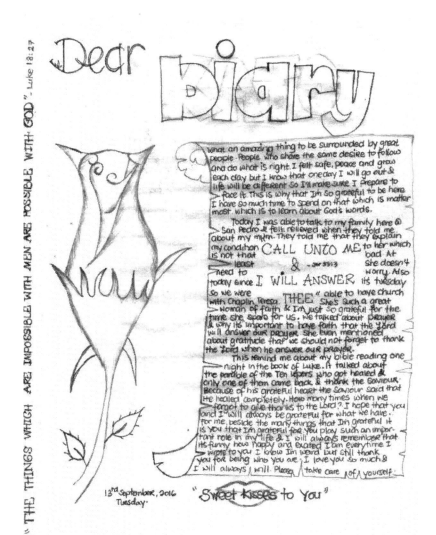

"THE THINGS WHICH ARE IMPOSSIBLE WITH MEN ARE POSSIBLE WITH GOD". Luke 18:27

Dear biary

What an amazing thing to be surrounded by great people. People who share the same desire to follow and do what is right. I felt safe, peace and grow each day but I know that one day I will go out & life will be different So I'll make sure I prepare to face it. This is why that I'm so grateful to be here. I have so much time to spend on that which is matter most which is to learn about God's words.

Today I was able to talk to my family here @ San Pedro & felt relieved when they told me about my mum. They told me that they explain my condition CALL UNTO ME to her which is not that least & ...Jer 33:3 she doesn't need to I WILL ANSWER worry. Also today since it's tuesday So we were THEE" able to have church with Chaplin Teresa. She's such a great woman of faith & I'm just so grateful for the time she spare for us. We talked about prayer & why it's important to have faith that the Lord will answer our prayer. She even mentioned about gratitude that we should not forget to thank the Lord when he answer our prayer.

This remind me about my bible reading one night in the book of Luke. It talked about the parable of the Ten Lepers who got healed & only one of them came back & thank the Saviour. Because of his grateful heart the Saviour said that He healed completely. How many times when we forget to give thanks to the Lord? I hope that you and I will always be grateful for what we have. For me, beside the many things that I'm grateful it is you that I'm grateful for. You play such an important role in my life & I will always remember that It's funny how happy and excited I am everytime I wrote to you. I know I'm weird but still thank you for being who you are. I love you so much & I will always will. Please take care of yourself.

13rd September, 2016
Tuesday.

"Sweet Kisses to You"

Uncle Longo

---— ★ ★ ★ ———

One of the most important lessons I learned in jail was that joy required no time or location. If you choose it to be, now is the best time to be joyful. My skills improved by helping others in jail, patience grew, and love for these women took root in my heart. If I had waited until I was free to help others, I would have missed all my blessings. Undertaking a life of service made me a better version of myself. It enriched my relationships, gave me purpose, and the more I embodied the servant role, the easier my situation became.

One of my biggest joys came from Uncle Longo. He was the one who supported me in jail. Without him, I would have been lost. After deciding to fight for asylum, some family members tried to change my mind. "Deport yourself. You cannot stay there," they would say. Understandably, they didn't want me in jail and couldn't understand why I stayed. After hearing from them, I began to question my decision. I didn't have to suffer in jail. I could deport myself and be done with it all.

But Uncle Longo's visit that first weekend made me realize I needed to stay and fight for my life. He told me not to worry about anything and that he had my back. That was the one thing I needed to hear. I wasn't sure what jail would be like, but I knew I had him. At times, he was more concerned about me than I was. He was my blessing.

Many detainees had no help from the outside, and asylum is nearly impossible without someone outside. Without help, most detainees self-deported. Without my uncle's support, I know I would have gone back home to face whatever awaited me. He was there for me every document needed, every hearing arrangement, every word of comfort. I wished I could hug him when I saw him, but the shackles on my wrists and ankles prevented anything more than thoughts of gratitude from forming. I relied on him for my life. He was my lifesaver.

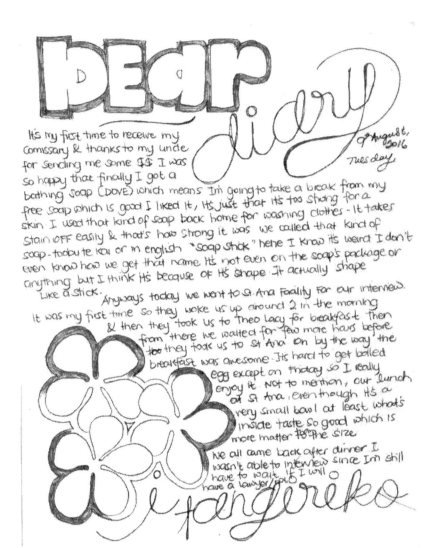

Dear diary

9th August, 2016
Tuesday

It's my first time to receive my comissary & thanks to my uncle for sending me some $$ I was so happy that finally I got a bathing soap (DOVE) which means I'm going to take a break from my free soap which is good I liked it, It's just that It's too strong for a skin I used that kind of soap back home for washing clothes - It takes stain off easily & that's how strong it was we called that kind of soap - toobu te kou or in english "soap stick" hehe I know its weird I don't even know how we get that name It's not even on the soap's package or anything but I think It's because of Its shape It actually shape like a stick. Anyways today we went to St. Ana Facility for our interview. It was my first time so they woke us up around 2 in the morning & then they took us to Theo Lacy for breakfast then from there we waited for few more hours before too they took us to St Ana on by the way the breakfast was awesome. It's hard to get boiled egg except on friday so I really enjoy it not to mention, our lunch at St Ana, even though It's a very small bowl at least what's inside taste so good which is more matter than the size

We all came back after dinner I wasn't able to interview since I'm still have to wait if I will have a lawyer/pro.

tangereko

Election Night 2016

The United States holds presidential elections once every four years. Election night is a night Americans stay up to watching results as they come in. Keen to observe, we also watched. By then, I had been in jail for three months and was kept abreast of the American political scene by deputies. With great interest, they watched each presidential debate.

All detainees were excited to see Hilary Clinton run. We related to her better than Donald Trump. She wanted to help people like us. People who weren't born rich knew how to work hard for the American dream. To us, America still represented a dream worth fighting for. We sought better lives. Some of us had families and wanted to be reunited with our loved ones. Hillary believed in dignity and the right to pursue the American dream. She was us. I loved how she believed in so many things that mattered. But, most importantly, we loved how she believed in the power of women.

Donald Trump was hostile. He always seemed to find the worst in others and was only concerned with himself. He wanted to deport all of us because, to him, we did not belong in America. To make America great again, we would have to be sent back to where we would be killed. At times he referenced the deportation of criminals, but we were all criminals, or at least we felt we were. Fearing what might happen if he was elected, we waited.

Initially, Hillary Clinton was leading. Everybody cheered as new numbers came in, but when lights out came, the TV was turned off. That night, we went to bed filled with hope, awaiting headlines reading President-elect Hillary Clinton the following day.

As we came back from breakfast, we overheard officers discussing Donald Trump's victory. Many detainees were crying. We were devastated, not knowing what would happen to us. We prayed for comfort and peace, the two things we desperately needed. Several placed calls to their families, sharing how they felt and what might happen to them. Everyone asked their families to be prepared for anything. It was a sad day.

Detainees kept asking officers if they would be deported. "Stay calm, stay calm. Nothing immediate is going to happen. Donald Trump is not the President yet." Trying to reassure us, most worried.

American Asylee

How could Donald Trump be the new President when it seemed Hillary would be the president when we went to sleep? Officer Juan explained what we didn't see, and though Hillary lost the election, inside our hearts, she won. All of us looked up to her for her belief in others, her experiences around the world, and most importantly, her faith in women.

Court Days

★ ★ ★

Court days were the only days you traveled to Santa Ana or Los Angeles. They were special days that could either be good or bad. Women would put their hair in fancy braids and thread their eyebrows with bedsheet fibers. On my court days, my African friends braided my hair in unique and intricate styles. We traded jail clothes to get better-fitting outfits for appearances. For some reason, the officers never noticed. Maybe because it was early, and they were ready to go home after a long night.

We were woken between 2:00 - 2:30 a.m. by an on-duty officer. With only a few minutes to wash our faces, brush our teeth, and collect our paperwork, we rushed to make the transport call outside. Pre-court nights were used to fix our appearance since there was no time in the morning. You were lucky if other female detainees joined you; otherwise, it was just you with a bunch of males.

Before stepping out of the building, deputies inspected us to make sure we didn't bring anything other than what was needed for court. Once cleared, we walked towards the line of armored busses and got shackled by sheriffs before entering. If traveling with a companion, both shared one set of handcuffs and sat together. The bus ride took between twenty and thirty minutes, depending on the traffic.

We waited in a jail cell for several hours at our first stop. Sometimes brown-bagged breakfasts awaited us on the ground, and officers would pass them to us. Long rides from the facility to Los Angeles were always a treat. If lucky, we sat in the front of the bus and saw all the things we didn't get to see in detention.

The freedom that came with court days always felt refreshing, even if only for a few hours. We listened to music that reminded us of better times on these trips. Males usually sang along with rap songs. When artists like Taylor Swift came on, I sang along in my heart and enjoyed every second. It reminded me of times spent with my friends and family in London, Australia, America, and Kiribati. Those hours, music was our therapy. Sometimes, a driver would sense joy and turn up the volume. Other drivers would immediately change the channel to remind us we were criminals.

I would wait in the same room I stayed in when apprehended at the airport. The room had a small TV mounted on the wall, two phones, and a small metal platform running across the perimeter. No adult could lie on this platform comfortably. The cold metal, combined with our thin jail clothes, added to the discomfort of the room. During the winter months, the guards gave us a light sweater.

Despite the cold, I always looked forward to these days. It was the food that made these days memorable. Typical meals in jail included four slices of bread, one fruit (apple or orange), one packet of mayonnaise, and mustard with two small cookies. At court, lunches varied. Sometimes we received a cheeseburger or Chinese takeout with extra cookies and milk.

When it was time, officers would bring me from the waiting cell and place me with other detainees. Then, cuffed and shackled, we walked in a single file line to the courtroom. Being restrained and paraded around made me feel like a real criminal. I imagine free people wouldn't feel safe around me. I understood the protocol, but it still broke my heart to be chained. The trip from the waiting cell to the court always felt longer than it was because of the chains. The shackles were so heavy, and sometimes they hurt my feet. Nevertheless, I remained quiet and endured the pain as I walked.

In the courtroom, I would see family. My uncle always waited outside the courtroom for me. I sensed an overwhelming amount of sadness each time I saw him. I would smile and try to ease his worry by letting him know

I was okay and happy to see him. I wanted to hug him, but the shackles and officers prevented this.

Hearings always began with public declarations of why we entered the United States. At first, I was embarrassed to share my story in front of everyone; but I became used to it after a few court appearances.

The court was a formal setting where respect must be given, especially to the judge and lawyers. As a non-native speaker, I was nervous, especially when representing myself. My hands shook as I held the microphone. My voice quivered. I worried about saying something that would negatively impact my case. Every unrepresented detainee had these same worries. If lucky, they had time to find legal representation. However, many did not understand English and stood before the judge in silence.

Some questions were easy, and some were not. The better prepared you were, the better chance you had to win asylum. The first hearing was always about your worthiness for asylum. Then, if you got lucky, another hearing was scheduled. If not, deportation was set by the end of the day.

Once court finished, we were led back to the holding cells to await transport back to jail. As the only female, I would often return to the cold cell in solitary confinement until dinner arrived in a brown bag. Always a surprise, I looked forward to these treats before boarding the bus back to jail.

My Love Diary

6th October, 2016
Thursday

Today I supposed to have my lawyer with me at court but for some reason she didn't turn up so the Judge didn't give me more time but just start right away with my case. I knew that I don't have much choice so all I need to do is to be respectful & answer the question politely.

Gladly it went well since she was able to give me my asylum form which I need to turn in on my next court on the 3rd of Nov. There are some cases where the denied an asylum so I'm grateful she didn't deny mine.

After my court finished, I went & wait for almost 8 hours for the bus to take us back to our facility. At first it was hard to wait for such a long time but now I'm glad I'm kinda get used to it. At the waiting room I was able to meet with Alejandra from St. Barbara jail & she just appreciate every food that we got that day. Not only that but we were able to talk about the things that we appreciate now that we used to take granted before. This is one of my favourite thing to do to see & learn the things that I get to learn only in this place. My freedom doesn't really matter to me before until I got into this place & realize how freedom is a gift & a blessing.

Finally we come back a bit late & thanks to the other detainees for their entertainment it was fun we get to know each other & the places were from especially the different language we spoke. When I came back, the other girls are so amazed that my next court will be in a month & so it looks like I will get a bond hearing before I finish my case with Nunez but we'll see cause you never know what's gonna happen. That's one of the things that I learnt from my experience that anything can happen you just gotta prepare to face it.

Since it's the last page of the first pad I just wanna say how grateful I am for your love. Eventhough I don't know what's going on with you right now but still I'm grateful that at one point you love me & you right now but still I'm grateful that for the first time loving someone that mean something. And to be honest for the first time loving someone push me to change my heart & not only that but also to push me to act upon my love for you to write to you everyday no matter how busy or how tired I am & I'm still going to write. Anyways as always I love you so much & I miss you too please take care !!

DEAR Diary

27ᵗʰ September, 2016
Tuesday

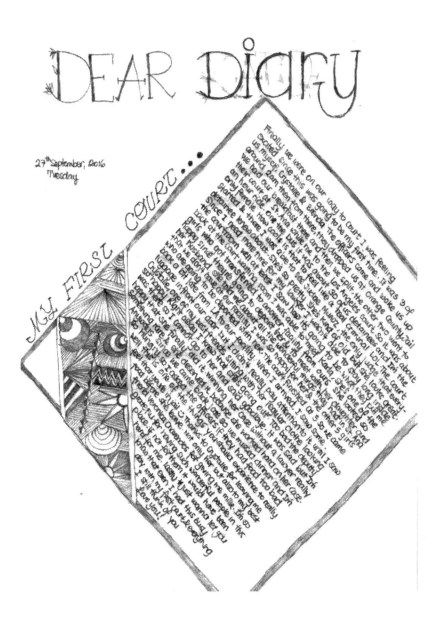

MY FIRST COURT...

The Fighter

— ★ ★ ★ —

One of my best friends called her *the fighter*. She was terrific at arguing and always came up with justifications to make others feel they were wrong. She only smiled and showed kindness when she needed something. Sometimes people believed she was genuine, but she returned to her cruel ways after getting what she wanted.

I knew the fighter well; she was my block-mate. There was no one physically closer to her in the entire jail, and I felt sorry for her. But the more disturbing her behaviors became, the more I hated her. Whenever she asked someone for help, I judged her. I'd seen it all before. I could predict the outcome of almost every interaction. Sometimes I was wrong, but most of the time, I was right.

What I didn't realize was how much she also controlled my behavior. I was filled with hatred when I was around her. I became unhappy with myself. The more negativity I saw, the less I wanted to help. I became hyper-judgmental. Mother Teresa once said, "if you judge people, you have no time to love them." And yet, I couldn't help but judge her. I focused on her flaws and mistakes. She controlled my perspective. I needed to refocus my attention on her positive aspects. When I did, I began to see how beautiful she was.

Her only friend was a detainee everyone despised; many thought she had mental problems. Despite this, the fighter treated her as her own and even called her cousin. They were an odd couple, but their friendship proved how lovely a person she was. After noticing this, I began talking to her and offering compliments. It surprised her. Her face lit up, and out of nowhere, a thank you. I'd praise her hair or the way she colored her pictures, and each time, she replied with the prettiest smile and a sincere thank you. We weren't the best of friends, but from the minute I decided to see her for her, I enjoyed her presence, and I hoped she enjoyed mine.

The gift of time

★ ★ ★

I never had as much free time in my life as I had in jail. I worried about so many things on the outside. Always occupying myself with things of little to no importance, I was addicted to social media. It was how I kept in touch with home, for better or worse. It wasn't terrible, but it didn't add much value to my life. I never had to worry about that in jail. I accepted things as they were and found freedom in seclusion. Initially, the separation from friends was hard, but separation from my mom was the hardest. One of her letters told me not to worry about them. They were fine, and they understood my situation. Her words helped, but I still worried.

In my culture, the eldest child has the greatest responsibility. With my younger siblings still in school and an unemployed father, I always felt the need to step up. I did this for nearly two years before escaping Kiribati. In her letter, my mom said she always knew I was strong, and everything would work out. She always believed in me and knew exactly what to say.

Waiting in jail, I could use my time wisely or waste it lamenting over my situation. Without question, I wanted to be wise, but how?

Some women sought advice from me and wanted to learn how I stayed so happy. They wanted to find happiness. But, unfortunately, many only saw the bad. I thought if I could share insight with others on how to stay positive in jail, maybe I would have served my purpose.

My aunt lived roughly six hours away from the jail. Visiting me was difficult, but she managed to come one time. I looked up to her and was so grateful for the visit. I remember watching her as she entered. I was glad to see her but also ashamed. She smiled as our eyes met. Out of embarrassment, I laughed. I was nervous, but she immediately calmed my nerves when she told me she was proud of me. "I applaud you for what you're doing. Fighting for your case instead of giving up and going back home is the right thing to do." I couldn't believe what I was hearing. "Eventually," she said, "you could write a book about your experience." My heart jumped as she continued. "This is America; anything is possible." At first, I thought she was crazy. Someone like me, who barely passed her English class in high school, could write a book?

Her words were like seeds in my mind. I started to think about it. *What if I did write a book?* I knew it would be difficult, but at the same time, I knew it was possible. She was correct; I was in America, where anything was possible. So I began looking for books on how to write books. Excitement overwhelmed me as I thought about the stories I would tell. I began writing whatever came to mind.

Day one was difficult. I re-wrote the first paragraph at least thirty times. I didn't give up, though. I continued until I completed one full page. *Not bad for a first-timer,* I thought.

Fellow detainees expressed heartfelt sorrow as my case kept getting postponed, month after month, but I saw delays as opportunities to add more experiences to my book. The writing was hard. There were days and weeks I felt I couldn't do it. I watched an episode of my favorite show during one of these periods, which reignited my inspiration.

It was April 24, 2017, when the Ellen Show hosted Sheryl Sandberg, author of *Option B.* Sheryl explained how she used her most challenging life experience, the loss of her husband, to help others overcome challenges in their own lives. The show reignited my flame and renewed my purpose. As she talked, I heard my voice inside hers – the pain, difficulties, and sorrow. This was my life! The only difference was she used her challenges to inspire others. I felt like she spoke directly to me, telling me exactly what I needed to do.

Realizing I could be in jail for an indefinite amount of time, I had to keep writing. I had to keep my perspective and see jail as an opportunity. Seeing the good in my situation kept me going. When extra time was added to my detainment, I chose to work harder on the things I wouldn't have done if I freed. Time allowed me to read inspirational books for a future manuscript. I wanted to use my life for others, reach out to women worldwide living in abusive relationships and assure them that there was a way out!

The more my case was delayed, the more time I had to work on a book. Another day, another page. In jail, all I had was time. I had lived through so many years of unhappiness that jail was a kind of stable relief. I was safe, I had friends, and I had food. I was happy. My secret to happiness was an attitude of gratitude. Each day, each hour, each minute. Gratitude.

I began sharing this secret and steps to gratefulness. They were the same steps I brought with me to the Philippines.

- Come what may and love it.
- Learn from difficulties and become stronger.
- See things not as adversities but as opportunities.
- How you choose to react to adversity dictates your happiness.

- Approach adversity with positivity.
- Instead of getting angry, laugh.
- Choose to be happy and kind.

I practiced these tips daily and encouraged others to practice as well.

Hungry

★ ★ ★

Random inspections were another thing I feared in jail. Deputies would rush in, demanding us to vacate our bunks. Sometimes we were moved to the dayroom. Other times, the yard. The most common breaches were food violations. This may seem trivial, but to us, it was huge. We were warned, placed on a watch list, or punished if violations were discovered. Every random search created panic. Our belongings were searched to ensure no extra slices of bread or additional pieces of fruit were hidden in our beds. Chinese detainees were commonly cited for having personally made books and ornaments. They loved making crafts from scrap pieces of brown paper. Deputies targeted specific blocks because of this.

LINE UP! FACE THE WALL! NO TALKING!

We lined so as not to see inspections. Concern grew as we heard the room being torn apart. Bedsheets, pillows, and whatever personal property we had was tossed on the floor. Standing, we whispered. *Did you remove that extra bread I gave you? Did you throw away that extra orange?* Every time we heard, *Oh, no!* We knew that someone had been busted. Once you were caught with contraband, there was no way to escape the consequences.

After inspections were finished, we returned to our beds and fixed what had been torn apart. Those with contraband found notes on their beds. Sometimes deputies would call bunk numbers. When this happened, individuals reported for punishment immediately.

We didn't want to break the rules, but we had to at times. We kept extra bread for when we got hungry at night. We made notebooks from lunch bags to teach English to non-English speakers.

One night, after inspection, I was asked to report. I'd been sick that day, so my friends gave me an extra orange. Usually, I ate all the extra food before night so that I wouldn't get caught. Unfortunately, on this night, I was too sick. I had forgotten entirely about the orange, but I remembered during the inspection and was afraid. I didn't want to get in trouble since all activity in jail was reported to your asylum judge. Fortunately, I was given a warning and let back into the day room. After that, I made sure I never had an incident again.

A lot of food was thrown away after every inspection. But one hiding spot that seemed safe was inside an empty bed. For some reason, the officers only checked occupied bunks. Empty bunks were our go-to's. Mealtimes were 5:00 a.m., 11:00 a.m., and 4:30 p.m. Most of us were still full from lunch when dinner was served, so we didn't eat dinner when we should have, resulting in nighttime hunger. Hidden slices of bread were most precious at night. It was the only food that stopped our stomachs from growling. For those who could afford them, Ramen noodles were detainee currency. Services like threading eyebrows, braiding hair, or even doing chores could be purchased with noodles.

No matter how clear the rule was, all of us ignored it. We needed food to survive and to sleep. We couldn't sleep on empty stomachs. So most nights, everyone got up at least once to go to the fountain. Needing food, we drank water. The only solution to hunger was commissary, a jail store filled with everything from soaps to snacks but getting items from the commissary was a luxury. Only detainees with access to money could afford such things.

Hunger forced most to break every rule just to eat. It was sad living in fear while doing the things we did to survive. But, living in jail makes you see things differently.

Whispers traveled like the flu whenever someone noticed even the slightest hint of inspection. Contraband was hidden in safe places, a trash can in the restroom, or an empty bed. You learned the meaning of conspicuous movements. Discreetly, detainees would make their way to the bathroom, where wrapped slices of bread would slowly find their way into the trash. Disgusting, maybe, but we did what we had to do.

Those who didn't make it to the bathroom in time took care of their food in other ways. Some wrapped fruit and bread in plastic, passing it to detainees close to empty beds — hoping to recover their food later that night. This is how we survived incarceration.

Spice it up!

* ★ *

Happiness is loving what you have

We didn't have much in jail, but we did have creativity. The repetition of fruit and bread wore on us, but we had to be thankful for what we received. Food from the commissary was also limited, mostly just snacks and ramen noodles. In jail, those were gold. Everybody, no matter how often they ate it, loved ramen. Our Chinese friends made the best ramen. They added ingredients from the commissary to spice it up. Some days, they pooled enough money to purchase pork snacks; other days, they bought Cheetos. I bet you never knew Cheetos could elevate ramen to the next level. Cooking in jail was an art form. Whatever they chose to add created so much flavor! Sometimes you couldn't even tell it was ramen. They made salads from grass collected in the yard, and with condiments, it was almost like eating salad in a restaurant!

Our Latina friends made tortilla magic. They would put all sorts of stuff inside to make their creations taste like tacos from a taco truck. The only thing missing was meat.

But, creativity didn't stop with food. We created beauty products and crafts with what we had. Some used the brown paper from the commissary to create intricate art pieces.

Before confiscating their work, detainees decorated their shelves with paper swans or birds, sometimes just for a few minutes. Others created beauty products: face moisturizer, eyeliner, and makeup. Some women would take extra milk and mix it with daily allotments of lotion from the facility to make face moisturizer. The moisturizer made your face feel cleaner and smoother than the expensive moisturizer sold in the commissary.

We learned how to spice up our lives in jail. All attempted to make our situation better with things like this. It took our minds off the outside and helped us embrace our lives inside detainment.

Haitian refugees

———— ★ ★ ★ ————

A deputy walked into the dayroom one morning to give us a heads up. "There will be new detainees soon. There are a lot, so we will need help from all of you to set them up with a new bed and welcome them to the facility." Everyone was excited! New detainees meant more bodies to warm the rooms. Even in the summer, the jail was cold. More detainees also meant more people to play card games with and have conversations in the yard. We looked forward to their arrival.

One after another, they kept coming. It was the first time any of us ever saw so many at once. One stood out. She was taller than our tallest guard and larger than our sheriff. She was intimidating. Her face looked angry, and she refused to speak to anyone. Her name was Ale.

Once all were in, the guards called out names and assigned beds. Everyone moved to help the new detainees.

Eve was one of the youngest to enter. She smiled, telling me how excited she was to get a bed finally. *How long has it been since you last slept,* I asked? "Nine days," she replied. "It was too cold to fall asleep on the trail, and there were no clouds to keep us warm. So we had to keep walking to make it to the border before we froze to death." I felt sad and happy for her at the same time. She was so pleased to be with us at such a tragic cost.

But not everyone was like Eve. Some were angry and didn't want to be here. Misinformed by family members residing in the United States, it seemed a few traveled great distances, not finding a better life as they hoped, rather jailed with the rest of us. Some were told they could live with their relatives already here once they crossed the border. Now detained, they would wait. If their hearing went well, they would get what they sought. If not, they faced deportation. All of us faced the same situation.

The room filled with conversations as everyone introduced themselves to each other. Groups gathered to fix beds while others balked at the living conditions. The mattresses were not thick, and the jail only allocated two thin white sheets for each bed. It was all we had. I can't remember how many times my blankets caused my skin to break out in hives, but it was something I learned to live with.

After twenty minutes, the dayroom opened. Some went to the TV while others went to the phones and showers. My new friends and I decided to watch a movie. We were about halfway through the film when we heard someone crying. It was Ale. Her bunkie reported her for smelling bad and refusing to shower. Deputies summoned her to the office.

Wiping tears from her eyes, she returned a short time later. Soon after, my number was called. I wondered why I was being called. I proceeded into the office where several deputies had gathered.

They explained Ale's situation and asked if I would be her new bunkie. I was happy, too, since I didn't have a bunkie. They thanked me and told me to be kind to her since it was her first day. I went to my bed and asked Eve if she would help me with Ale's stuff. Ale only spoke French Creole, so communication was a challenge. When Ale came, I helped her set up her bed. I tried to talk to her, but of course, she didn't understand anything.

That night as I wrote in my gratitude journal, I felt the bunk move. Ale sobbed below. It was typical that new detainees cried during their first night. Many pleaded out loud for help. Yet, we were not allowed to make a sound and felt helpless watching them cry.

The following day, I tried to show her how much I cared, not through words but by actions. One of the many challenges in jail is having enough food to eat, but if someone had money, they could buy snacks from the commissary. Luckily, I had some extra food that day. I put a cup of ramen and a cookie on her shelf before going to shower. When I came back, both were gone. Pointing to

Ale, Evelyn said, "She wanted to tell you thank you." I smiled and asked Eve to tell Ale that she could ask me for anything, and I would help if I could.

Later that night, standing for the count, my new bunkie walked towards me. She took my ID in her hand and looked closely at it. "Grace?" I nodded my head and stood on my tippy toes with her ID in my hand, "Ale?" Nodding her head, she smiled. I was so happy to see her smile. We couldn't understand each other, but we knew we would get along just fine that night.

***

The next morning, I went to the shower. As always, it was crowded. Most preferred morning showers, and since we never knew when the showers would close, it was always best to grab a shower early. We had no clocks, so everyone had to get up early and move quickly to make roll call. My bunkie, three other ladies, and I were first that morning. I noticed my bunkie having trouble reaching her back with the soap. I offered to help. As I washed her back, every eye in the shower turned to us. I'm not sure if it was because they never saw light-skin before or if seeing a woman scrub another woman's back was strange. Back home, this was normal. Sometimes we showered in groups, especially when it rained. We helped each other, so helping her didn't bother me.

Immediately, I was surrounded by three other hands holding soap. I ended up scrubbing a few more backs that morning. It was funny and sweet to see strangers willing to ask for help in this situation.

Sometimes, it's the simple things that make our lives meaningful. Scrubbing backs was a simple gesture, but it meant so much more. Not long after, Ale and I were great friends. On our first sheet rotation, Ale called me over to help her. She called me by a name I had never heard before. I asked Eve what it meant. "It means my mother. It's a sign of respect; she looks up to you." I was humbled and shocked hearing this. You would have thought the opposite if you saw us side by side. Ale was a beautiful giant compared to me. We shared food, danced, and became the best of friends.

Often, I would think to myself, *what if I never got the chance to be her bunkie? What if I only saw her as scary and dirty? Would I ever know the beautiful person she was? I don't think so.* But, my life was better because I was open to whatever came my way — and I loved it.

diary Mi Amor

I LOVE YOU SO MUCH!...

What a wonderful day starting with 15 new women came in from Haiti. I was so happy to see them at the same time I'm sad when I heard about their story on how they got here. They were all came from Brazil & they spend 5 months to travel & then 9 days to walk from Mexico to the border. Their experience made me grateful of of my life that I didn't struggle as they were. Sometimes we easily complained when things weren't going the way we wanted but if we compare our problems with the other people especially in Africa it is nothing so we need to be grateful for everything we have & went through. I was able to meet my new neighbor, her name is Evelyn & she's one of the nicest & funny girl I ever met. All of my friends were mocking me that I'm the same with Evelyn. Most of her friends that she came with were crying & some were mad. But her? She's so happy & she laughed when someone trying to talk to her in English since she doesn't understand English. She's just amazing & grateful she can be my neighbor. It was a fun & busy day for all of us @

JMF

- 99 -

Service

* ★ *

Half of God's commandments are about valuing
relationships with others. I believe this is an essential
part of his plan. We are all his children, and he wants
us to work together to bring out the best in all.

Back home, I was a teacher. I taught information technology classes for almost two years before running away. Teaching others was the first thing that came to mind when I changed my jail perspective. Most detainees did not speak English or even attend school. I was different. I had attended university in Fiji and the United States. Though I still struggled with English, I knew how to read, write, and converse in English. Many fellow detainees wanted to learn English, so I decided to use my skills to make English classes.

On my first day of instruction, only two showed up. I made flashcards and phrase sheets for them, and both seemed to enjoy it. Interest grew as more heard about the class. Within a couple of weeks, the small group had grown. The English class turned into much more. We started sharing stories of how each of us ended up here.

Now, I'd always thought my circumstances were bad but listening to their stories made my experiences seem trivial. When I first saw Solange, a friend from Cameroon, I assumed she had no major problems other than being in jail with me. She had a beautiful smile and such a positive spirit. Like me, she fled her country, fearing for her life. She climbed mountains, crossed lands riddled with human remains, and eventually made her way here.

Solange's Story

I had no idea what awaited me as I entered Darien Jungle. I believed the trip would not be difficult since I felt so good on my first day. I was utterly wrong. At the beginning of my journey, I was accompanied by nine men seeking better futures. Our goal was to get to Panama, but we did not know how to get there. We hoped we might find someone to show us the way.

We met fellow migrants who gave up and decided to return on our way. They told us they could not find their way to Panama and decided the safety of the camp was better than the jungle. That's when I began to worry and realized that the trip would not be as easy as I thought. Despite this, we walked. It was the longest walk of my life. We climbed high mountains. It was difficult for me. I was the only woman in the group. One of the men collapsed, and I freaked out. I thought if he could collapse, surely, I would too. It was hard to stay with the men, and I was left behind in the end. Finally, one was kind enough to stay back with me. He knew that there was no way I could make it on my own. We walked together, and my feet could not take any more steps at one point. I had no choice. I needed to rest. That man told me that I needed to lighten my bag to make the trip easier. I pulled out some clothes but kept my blanket to keep me warm at night. The following night, we started our journey again. It is risky to travel at night, but it was better than moving in the heat. We did not have food, only water.

After hours of walking, we decided to take a rest. We found ourselves stuck on one big rock surrounded by water. We had no choice other than to sleep on that rock. That night, I prayed for protection. We slept safely, and when both of us woke, we continued our trip to the other side of that water. On the way, we saw so many corpses and skeletons. It was not easy. People died trying to do what we were doing. It was sad and scary at the same time. It was so hot. I wanted to give up.

I got sick. I thought there was no way I could continue. I had a fever, and my feet were swollen from the water. I kept taking off my boots to cool my feet. It was hard when we came to an area without any water, but of course, I could not take off my boots. The jungle was full of snakes. Those days in the wilderness felt like forever. The struggle was real.

My friend encouraged me to be strong and keep walking. Up to a point, I did it with his help until we came to a steep and rocky mountain. By this time, we had other guys with us. They also were trying to go to Panama. Halfway up the mountain, I felt weak. My body could hardly make it. I asked the man ahead of me to give me his hand for support. He refused. By this time, everyone had trouble climbing, but I hoped he would help me, the only female. I had a line of people behind me. If I stopped, everyone behind me would stop. Luckily one guy found his way to me and began pulling me up. He was a strong man, and he saved my life. After we reached the other side of the mountain, we decided to rest.

Three people approached us soon after laying down, asking for money. They seemed nice, so I slowly took cash from my bra. When they saw I had money, they threatened us and told us to take off our clothes. I was so scared. I quickly said a prayer. I didn't want to get raped or killed. Fortunately, after they got what they wanted, we were left alone. I began wondering if I would ever make it out of that jungle alive or just become another corpse on the path. I kept going.

The only thing I had left with me was my faith in God. He would be the one to take care of me, no matter what. But, I also came to realize that faith needed action. I could not just wait for the Lord to bring Panama to me; I had to walk the distance, climb the mountains, and endure my sickness. But, no matter how much I suffered, physically and emotionally, God would eventually bring me out of that jungle, wholly healed.

***

Hearing Solange's story made me respect her even more. Her courage, bravery, strength, and heart amazed me. How many women like her have traveled to be here, knowing the price they would pay? Solange's experience and other detainees made me realize that being an asylum seeker was not something to be ashamed of. On the contrary, I am proud to be an asylum seeker. We have courage, strength, and ferocious desires for better lives. We are the ones we have been waiting for!

Years of affliction ate away at who we used to be. Our souls should be filled with anger, and resentment but they aren't — at least not entirely. Nights were always the most challenging parts in jail. Women cried about court date postponements, deportation, loneliness, hunger, and sadness. Yet, despite this, there was joy.

We would talk about our favorite foods in the courtyard and how we planned to eat them when we got out — tamales from Mexico, fish, and rice from Kiribati, or noodle soup from China. Remembering smells, tastes, colors, and textures made our mouths water and stomachs growl. We laughed and cried, thinking about the foods we missed from home. It was moments like these that made us family.

We had each other, and because of them, I enjoyed detainment. I made friends. I developed strong relationships, and I began feeling good about myself again. Most importantly, I started seeing God's blessings again. I began to live each day purposefully, and everything I did was towards a greater purpose. In those walls, I found hope; I prayed, loved, and lived.

***

Fighting for asylum is hard. It's even more difficult when you don't have any support from the outside. Without assistance, documents don't get filed, court dates are missed, and detainments are prolonged. Everyone in detention needs a lawyer, and lawyers cost money. For some, this means expedited deportation to the country they fled. For others, waiting for pro bono lawyers can add months to years of detainment. I understood English, read, and had legal help on the outside. My lawyer showed me how to file forms. It was a simple process.

Realizing these women needed help, I began completing asylum applications for each one of them. To me, the form was a simple piece of paper, but to them, it was much more. I saw hope in their eyes each time they received a completed form. Helping my asylum sisters was a humbling experience. They needed me as much as I needed them. I loved serving and getting closer to each one I supported.

I gained the trust and respect of my fellow detainees from this simple act of service. The correctional officers took note and appointed me to a house mouse position. House mice were charged with helping guards organize detainee chores and activities. Because of my desire to help others, everyone in the facility seemed happy to help me, making my house mouse responsibilities easier. It's true; what goes around comes around.

My Love
Hello

23rd October, 2016

HAPPY SABBATH DAY ♡

"I've been thinking a lot about my life & the people that I have in my life & it made me realize how blessed I am. The Lord blessed me through many things. So it's time for me to repay Him through obedience & service to His children especially here in this Jail."

"Today since no class, some of the Haiti women asked if they can join my english class tomorrow I was so happy that I will have 4 new students plus the other 3 chinese ladies"

"IT'S NEVER TOO LATE ∞
OR TOO EARLY TO FULFILL YOUR DREAM"

"I'm just grateful for being here having so many opportunities to serve other people. Not only that but I'm so thankful for the Lord's love and for people's prayer that really helped me so much here. So far this time only few days those I missed my family but the rest I'm just happy getting to know great woman in this place. Not just that but it gives me desire to improve myself in different areas includes exercise, diet, spanish & more I just a grateful for the wonderful things I learnt here."

"I would say the dinner today is the Bomb I really liked it and so as the other ladies it was wonderful and we just grateful for those who prepare & pay for it"

Te Amo Mi Amor!

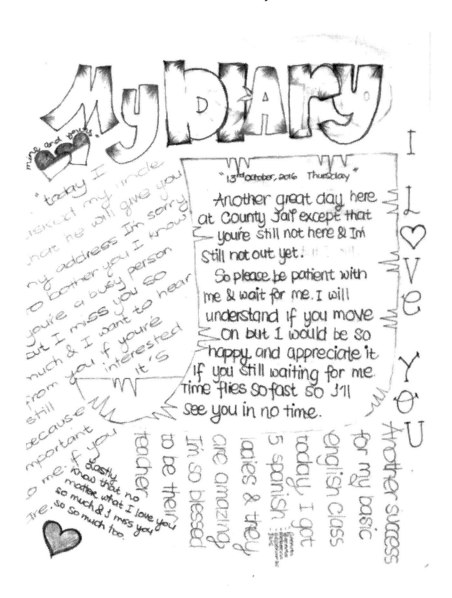

My Diary

"today I asked my uncle what he will give you my address. I'm sorry to bother you. I know you're a busy person but I miss you so much & I want to hear from you if you're interested it's still because important you me. If lastly know that no matter what I love you so much & I miss you are. So so much too.

"13th October, 2016 Thursday"

Another great day here at County Jail except that you're still not here & I'm still not out yet.

So please be patient with me & wait for me. I will understand if you move on but I would be so happy and appreciate it if you still waiting for me. Time flies so fast so I'll see you in no time.

teacher to be their I'm so blessed are amazing ladies & they 5 spanish today, I got english class for my basic Another success

I LOVE YOU

The spirit of Christmas

When in jail, the last thing you want to think about is Christmas. A season spent with friends and family, people so near and dear to you that Christmas without them just isn't Christmas.

It was early September when I began thinking about Christmas. At first, I kept it to myself. I didn't want my friends to think I was crazy. Who celebrates Christmas in jail? But, I couldn't get the thought out of my mind. I loved Christmas, and the idea of doing something to celebrate wouldn't leave my mind. It came to mind in the shower, in the yard, in bed, everywhere.

The sun was shining, birds were chirping, and the sound of vehicles speeding by on the Alton Parkway always reminded me that there was more out there than in here. My friends and I would gather underneath the shade of a magnificent tree to enjoy lunch. We didn't have much, but we had each other, which was more than enough. We shared news from letters received. Any communication from the outside was like gold. When there was no more to share, I spoke up. I wasn't worried about being seen as crazy any longer, and to my surprise, everyone was excited to help make it a reality. Leah came up with decoration ideas, and Juliet proposed buying treats from the commissary. Brianna suggested we prepare Christmas songs; we loved singing.

Sometimes we would get too loud during lunches. Our laughter would drown out the distant sounds of traffic. I loved these moments. It didn't matter that we were incarcerated, that none of us had seen our families in months or even years; we had each other, and that's all that mattered. In these moments, we enjoyed life.

***

Miraculously, I completed the individualized gifts for everyone a few weeks before the celebration. However, I still needed to prepare extra gifts for the detainees without commissary.

I spent much of my allowance on Christmas gifts but thought it would be good to provide extra gifts for the new women. As I calculated the cost, I realized that even with help from my friends, we wouldn't be able to afford everything. I needed help from the outside. I asked our church leader for help. She always said she enjoyed helping others, but I was worried my request was too much.

I discussed the idea with my prayer group, and all supported it. I wrote a letter and asked everyone to sign. It remained tucked away in the Book of Genesis for two days. When Tuesday came, I brought my bible to the service and handed our letter to Maggie. Out of curiosity, I checked my balance a few days before Christmas. Maggie had deposited everything we asked for and more! Overjoyed, I shared the news with the group. We began making lists of items for the women.

***

Two days before the celebration, Leah and Juliet decided to make a Christmas tree out of a rotating book rack in the day room. We folded pieces of paper and decorated the rack to look like a tree. It was time-consuming, but with many helping hands, a tree was created! It was the most beautiful Christmas tree I had ever seen.

I wanted to provide a gift for each detainee but coming up with the right gift proved more difficult than I thought. Commissary only stocked certain items, and I didn't know each detainee personally. So, I raised the idea of making a secret sister gift exchange. I knew it would be a challenge with more than fifty women, but this was the only way to make it happen.

I worried some would get upset with the idea, but no one was. Instead, everyone wanted to know how they could get a gift for their secret sister. I suggested using the issued items we received from the facility and decorating them. Surprisingly, everyone was excited about the idea.

The day before Christmas was one of my busiest days in jail. My bed was full of paper and crayons. I made Christmas cones for specially ordered popcorn. Others were finishing their specially designed envelopes to hold their secret sister gifts.

***

On the day of the celebration, the smell of popcorn filled the day room. I wish I could say there was a fancier smell, but popcorn was all we could afford. The aroma of hot cocoa was added, putting everyone in a good mood. Understandably, some women did not join. I began questioning myself when I saw women resting in their beds while others sang, laughed, and ate. *Was this a good idea?*

Those celebrating kept asking, "Now what?" They were excited for more, and everyone saw me as the emcee. First up, Christmas carols. Many didn't know the lyrics, but the hymns were spot on! It touched my heart. All of us, separated from our families with little to share on Christmas, were celebrating.

In our native languages and some broken English, we sang as one. The songs were so moving that even those in their bunks walked out to see. Everyone had come together. After caroling, we played games. Laughter, love, joy was everywhere. Unfortunately, I missed all the games preparing for the gift exchange.

Placing each gift, I sensed the care, time, and effort spent on each one. When gifts were presented, secret sisters hugged, some laughed, and some cried — all with deep appreciation. It was the best Christmas in the loneliest place I've ever been.

That night as I laid my head down to sleep, I couldn't help but give thanks to God for making it happen. I believe God uses our desires and visions to direct us towards what we are intended for. I am convinced that we exist to serve each other, and that's why serving always feels good.

The following morning, I overheard a phone conversation between a detainee and her family. The excitement she expressed about the previous night's celebration was palpable. At that moment, I realized the celebration went far beyond our walls. It included families on the outside. They must have been shocked to hear how we partied in jail.

***

Our last planned surprise happened on Christmas morning. For the first time, detainees without commissary would have their shelves filled with items. The money Maggie donated allowed us to fill shelves not only on Christmas morning but throughout the entire Christmas week! Waking up, the women were shocked to see their shelves filled with items. All were thankful. Some even cried because of Maggie's Christmas miracle.

Like ripples of water from a stone, one small act of kindness can multiply into countless others. The Lord answered my prayer through my friends and gave me the courage to act on his special day. Who would have ever thought that one of my best Christmas memories would come from an American jail? Not I.

Dear Mi amor

Guess what? Well today my friends (spanish) called me to their group & told me that some of the new spanish women are excited about the plan that I had for xmas & they told me that they will contribute too to whatever I need from them I was so happy, I told them my plan & then tell them if they have other idea too. It's always a good feeling to know you have someone that you share same desire especially in helping other people. Before I thought that its hard but now I, don't think thats the case anymore. Its good to work in a group than by yourself Hopefully by tomorrow we will confirm what to do & to contribute for Xmas I have a great feeling that its gonna be great. I'm pretty sure that its the Lord that allowed these women to offer help & I'm just so grateful for them especially with a desire. He blessed me with Deep down I I know that I can't pull this thing by myself. Anyways I can't wait for xmas & see how everyone feels when they know that we will have a xmas morning program here at the James Musick Jail"

"Its funny today I was thinking about us being together finally thus is what happen when you think about someone every single day Anyways to be honest I would love to be with you in person

19th December, 2016
Mondays

Proverbs 27:1-2

"Do not boast about tomorrow for you DO not know what a day may bring Forth Let another man Praise you & not your own Mouth"

"It's the Action, not the fruit of the action, thats important. You have to do the right thing. It may not be in your power, may not be in your time, that there'll be any fruit. But that doesn't mean you stop doing the right thing. You may never know what results come from your action. But if you do nothing, there will be no result". - Gandhi

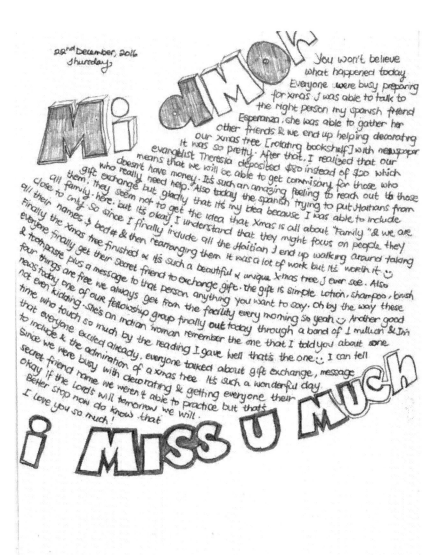

22nd December, 2016
Thursday,

Mi amor

You won't believe what happened today. Everyone were busy preparing for Xmas. I was able to talk to the right person my spanish friend Esperanza, she was able to gather her other friends & we end up helping decorating our Xmas tree [rotating bookshelf] with newspaper. It was so pretty. After that, I realized that our evangelist Theresia deposited $80 instead of $20 which means that we will be able to get commisary for those who doesn't really have money. It's such an amazing feeling to reach out to those who really need help. Also today the spanish trying to put Haitians from my family. here. but it's okay. I understand that Xmas is all about "Family" & we are gift exchange but gladly that it's my idea because I was able to include them, they seem not to get the idea that Xmas is all about "Family" & we are close to only. So since I finally include all the Haitian I end up walking around taking all their names & bed # & then rearranging them it was a lot of work but it's worth it ☺ Finally the Xmas tree finished & it's such a beautiful & unique Xmas tree I ever see. Also everyone finally get their secret friend to exchange gift. the gift is simple. lotion, shampoo, brush & toothpaste plus a message to that person anything you want to say. Oh by the way these four things are free we always get from the facility every morning So yeah ☺ Another good news today one of our fellowship group finally out today through a band of 1 million & I'm not even kidding. She's an Indian woman remember the one that I told you about some time who touch so much by the reading I gave well that's the one ⸫ I can tell that everyone excited already, everyone talked about gift exchange, message to include & the admiration of a Xmas tree. It's such a wonderful day. Since we were busy with decorating & getting everyone their secret friend name we weren't able to practice but that's okay if the Lords will tomorrow we will. Better stop now do know that I love you so much!

i MiSS U MUCH

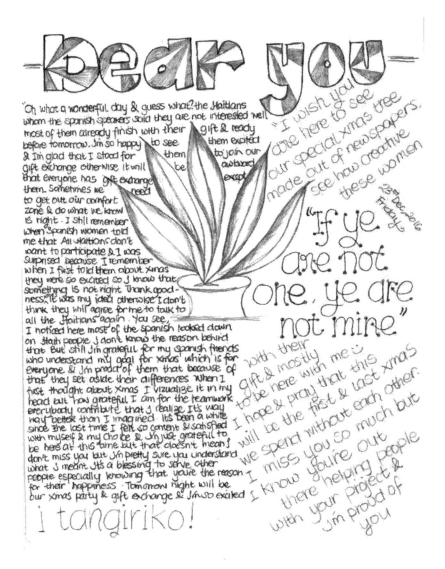

dear you

"Oh what a wonderful day & guess what? the Haitians whom the spanish speakers said they are not interested well most of them already finish with their gift & ready before tomorrow. Im so happy to see them excited & Im glad that I stood for them to join our gift exchange otherwise it will be awkward that everyone has gift exchange except them. Sometimes we need to get out our comfort zone & do what we know is right. I still remember when spanish women told me that All Haitians don't want to participate & I was surprised because I remember when I first told them about Xmas they were so excited so I know that something is not right Thank goodness. It was my idea otherwise I don't think they will agree for me to talk to all the Haitians again. You see, I noticed here most of the spanish looked down on Haiti people. I don't know the reason behind that But still Im grateful for my spanish friends who understand my goal for Xmas which is for everyone & Im proud of them that because of that they set aside their differences When I first thought about Xmas I visualize it in my head but how grateful I am for the teamwork everybody contribute that I realize It's way way better than I imagined Its been a while since the last time I felt so content & satisfied with myself & my choice & Im just grateful to be here at this time but that doesn't mean I don't miss you but Im pretty sure you understand what I meant. Its a blessing to serve other people especially knowing that you're the reason for their happiness Tomorrow night will be our Xmas party & gift exchange & Im so excited

¡ tangiriko !

"I wish you are here to see our special xmas tree made out of newspapers. see how creative these women

23th Dec 2016 Friday

"If ye are not one, ye are not mine"

with their gift & mostly to be here with me ☺ I hope & pray that this will be the first & last xmas we spend without each other. I miss you so much but I know you're out there helping people with your project & Im proud of you

My dearest

24th December, 2016
Saturday

I just don't know where to start or how to begin to describe this day [xmas celebration] anyways lets me start with the preparation that all of these amazing women did. It's just amazing. I'll tell you in person what I did but

"You will find, as you look back upon your life, that the moments that stand out are the moments when you have done things for others"
- Henry Drummond

I realized that it seems like I always bragged about myself to you lol but hope you understand how exited I am when it comes to helping people especially when I accomplish something.

Anyways finally all the gifts present under the xmas tree & its just a wonderful sight

TO be honest I'm crazy about you

Because it represent the desire of giving even if they're just regular envelope with different colors on top.

The popcorn cones are done & were ready. I can't tell you how different it is when it comes to reality compare to the plan you already had or even picture in your head. And I'm talking about 40 something old women with different situation. So yeah it was hard but since everybody seem to rely on me this time. I knew I have to be confident & not panic. It was hard since some refused to get off from their bed but of course I won't let that stop me to accomplish the puppy of this night that we already planned. Finally we started & again I conducted our choir. I notice that they most of them are nervous & kind of feel to offlined a bit but it doesn't matter to me because all it matters is that they all able to get the tune & sing infront of more than 40 women & thats something right after we finish. I noticed that more women started to come & say from far bad.

The night went on & all I can is that everyone enjoyed even the game & play drama was all funny & everything even though I'm busy & missed all of them while preparing popcorn for everyone & even I can tell that they all enjoy it. the noise was too loud and everyone participated. chinese, espanoles & haitian. The last part of course gift exchange & thats when I see the real joy came. everyone hugging and expressing their love & some are crying hope its a tear of joy but yeah it will be a night that I will always remember.

- Boyfriend

Letters of the heart

— ★ ★ ★ —

One of my favorite things in jail was receiving letters. It didn't matter who the letter was from or how long it was. The fact that someone remembered me always brought a smile to my face. Each time the deputy came with letters, excitement rose. We waited, hoping to hear our number. Knowing that someone took the time to write meant so much. Letters told us that someone out there was thinking of us, and we weren't alone in our quest for asylum.

***

Writing allows the author time to think about the message they want to convey to the reader. I cherished well-written, heartfelt letters of encouragement. There's something about the distance shared between thoughts, writers, and readers. Words seemingly gained power, traversing between freedom and incarceration. I found myself reading letters repeatedly, each time gaining deeper meaning.

No matter how bad my day was, receiving letters made everything better. Letters were an investment in time, and time, once spent, cannot be returned. To me, letters were the best gifts. The most powerful letters came from fellow detainees who were released on bond. More than anyone else's, their words encouraged me to keep fighting for asylum.

The following letter is from one of my best friends, Martha Nfoneh. My Christian fellowship leader from Cameroon won her case three months after meeting her in jail.

Hello Smiley,

I call you smiley because that's who you are, and you will never change from being that no matter the situation you are in. But, seriously, as I usually say, I admire you for always being so happy, polite, and encouraging others. You will be reading this letter when I am out of here, and I want you to know how much I love and miss you. You have been a wonderful friend to me. I will always cherish the times we shared. The memories will remain in my heart forever.

Graceful as your name, you need to thank God for revealing your name to your mum. I have never in my life seen anybody like you who laughs so hard, even when times are rough. I have never seen you raise your voice or get angry with anyone. Even when you are sad, it never shows. You have a beautiful soul. Thank you so much for putting up with me all this while. I know there are times I crossed the line. I didn't listen at times, and I am sorry if you were ever hurt. I know stubbornness is one of my weaknesses, and I pray God helps me out of it. Thank you for always trying to calm down the situation when we argue. It always helps me sleep at night. I pray for more patience with people and less stubbornness.

Thank you for being so selfless and loving. I will never forget you. I want you to know I have learned so much from you, especially in the prayer group. I will never forget the way we said goodnight to each other. When I had no food or calling cards, you provided them. Finally, I will never forget your plan for humanitarian organization for detainees.

Loves of love,

Martha

Knowing she found time to write as an asylum grantee motivated me to keep my spirits up and reassured me that I was not alone in my fight.

Forgiveness

— ★ ★ ★ —

Though here for many years, Tina had difficulty reading English. Older, she co-led our fitness group. A grandmother, she always wanted to read. Some nights we would practice with a book from the library. She would read, and I would correct her pronunciation. We would work hours each night. Her motivation was her grandchildren. She wanted to read to them when she got out of jail.

One day, she and another member of our Christian fellowship group got into an argument. Tina and Vero seemed to hate each other, and we didn't understand why. A week after the conflict began, our group leader decided it best we fast for them since praying had done nothing.

Several days of fasting, and still nothing. Their dislike for each other grew daily, and Vero stopped attending Bible study. Maggie encouraged us to continue praying for her. One day Vero was punished for hiding bread in her area. She was moved from the back to the front, making her new bed adjacent to mine. We had no problems and occasionally talked about our cases — she confided in me and I in her about our fears and worries of being denied. Then one night, as I sat on my bed, she whispered, "Grace, I need to tell you something." By the look in her eyes, I could tell whatever it was, was serious. Leaning over the edge of my bed, she said, "I hate her. Whenever I'm around her, I can tell she doesn't like me either. I don't like the way I feel. I miss Bible study, but I don't know what to do."

What happened? I asked. As she began sharing, I prayed for the right words to say. "There's no way I can forgive Tina, but I know our fight is hurting the group. Maybe it would be better if I left the group."

I paused, then responded. *Sometimes we think ignoring a problem is the best thing to do. We ignore conflict, hoping it will resolve on its own, but it never does.* I told her about a movie on adultery I watched several years before getting over my first marriage. The film taught me the importance of forgiveness. Holding onto grudges relinquishes power to the person who wronged us, and hate for that person controls us.

Do you know how I ended up here? I explained my problems at the airport. I told her about my friend who helped me with my ticket to America but didn't tell me that my return ticket wouldn't extend with my visa. When I realized the trouble I was in, I was upset, but my anger wouldn't fix the problem. I forgave her and prepared to face whatever came my way.

Forgiveness freed me of anger. I had more energy to focus on what mattered, a new beginning. As I finished my story, Vero was crying. She quietly thanked me for sharing and told me she was glad she shared. Keeping all this inside for weeks was hard. She felt better.

Words have power, and when delivered with love, they become even more. Later that week, Vero made her way to our line. I couldn't believe it. We had missed her for weeks. Finally, she was back!

Days later, I saw Vero approach Tina. Both sat and talked, then, out of nowhere, they hugged. The following day both were back in fellowship, sitting next to each other, and we were whole again.

Diary my dear

John 15:14
"You are my friend if you do whatever I command you."

pays off. Obedience always one of our fellowship member came to me and asked if I can help her. She's like two years older and she got 2 kids I immediately closed my book and start paying attention to her while she finally admitted the reason why she's been missing a fellowship for few days now. She started to tell me that she's offended by one of the women in our fellowship as she can't come again. Right there, I started to explain to her that she should forgive that person not for this person's sake but for her sake. It's like you're giving that person a grudge for someone else. Its like you're giving that person a power to control your life. Not only that but she let that person to stop her from getting the blessing from God. As I talked she was in tears and she told me that is exactly what she need to hear. She didn't realize that what she did worsen her situation. And guess what? well since tuesday meaning no fellowship but we have a church meeting & she finally joined. Seeing this lady coming makes me so happy & I'm grateful for the Lord for giving me this great opportunity. If it wasn't being a good example there is no way that this woman will approach me for help. I mean we have older women that are in our fellowship too but I'm grateful that she can trust me with her problem. This was the highlight of my day especially to know that you're a good influence in someone's life. It means so much to me.

Anyways, enough about me. Hows it going from your side? Everythings good? Any good news? How I wish that you can answer these right now so I stop worrying. How I wish that I'll just wait patiently until that day finally comes.

Do know that I love you so much & I miss you too. Goodnight & sweet dreams. Take care!

uhuuh !!

John 15:9-11
"Our Joy will Full If we keep his commandment"

1 Sam 15:22
"TO OBEY IS BETTER THAN SACRIFICE"

20th September, 2016
tuesday

"you're the cause of my JOY & HOPE" -GRACE 2 KATO

Visiting day

* ★ *

Once a week, Officer Frank would post a visitor signup sheet on the wall. Priority was given to those with no friends or family in the area. Visitors came from Friends of Orange County Detainees (FOCD). At first, I was excited about the opportunity. Most who signed up that week received a visitor, but I didn't. When given the opportunity again, I decided not to.

Contact with the outside was special. Visitors always brought excitement. All the detainees, except for Jennifer, waited for these days. She was from Honduras and crossed the border with her husband. Both were apprehended and separated. For a good reason, she always seemed sad or mad or both. She would begrudgingly stand up and go when called for visitation. When she returned, she was a different person. Like night and day, she would always come back smiling, laughing, talking, and happy. I always wondered who visited her? Who changed her? And how did they do it?

Jennifer mostly kept to herself, and to this day, I still do not understand what made her so happy. If visits from strangers could make the one person in our facility who hardly expressed any joy, I could only imagine the impact these visitors made on the thousands of other detainees throughout California.

*****

One day, an older lady from the organization interviewed me. She wanted to know how she could assist me. Asking if I ever signed up for a visit, I told her I did but was never selected.

I'm ok, though. I have regular visits from my uncle, I explained. She encouraged me to try again. So, not expecting anything, I signed up for a visit the following week and was shocked when Officer Joe called my name for a visit the following Thursday.

I sat in the visitor room, wondering who it would be. Then, I saw a beautiful woman waiting for me and asked if she was from FOCD. I first noticed her beautiful smile. Her kind spirit touched me from the other side of the room, knowing that she drove all this way to visit me. "Hi, Grace. I am Florence. I am from Friends of Orange County Detainees. How are you?" Our conversation blossomed into a discussion about her family and my situation. Thirty minutes went by so fast. Before leaving, Florence told me she would try to visit me each Friday. I was blessed to receive such a commitment from a stranger.

Florence continued to meet with me every Friday. We began knowing each other more and more. She shared what it was like being a FOCD volunteer and how volunteers gathered to share experiences. "Some volunteers talk about how bad their detainees have it and how sad it makes them feel," she said, "but you seem to be happy with detainment. I feel blessed to be with you. That is what I share."

What she said overwhelmed me. She was right, though. I was happy. I served others. Inside, I had a purpose I felt called to. The more I learned about her volunteer efforts, the more I wanted to be like her. She was at an age where she did not have to do anything, and yet she chose to be in jail with me. She was a super grandma with so much energy. Finally, I understood what made Florence so happy, FOCD kindness.

Jailbreak

★ ⭐ ★

August 9, 2017

I had been incarcerated for one year and two weeks when my final day came. I was the most tenured detainee in the entire ICE facility at the time. Many friends had left through bond or deportation. Those who went on bond awaited their hearings in the United States. I was happy for them but heartbroken for the ones deported. I recorded each case in my journal and marked each outcome when I heard the news. Those who won asylum were far fewer than those deported.

I became close to many women in jail. I helped file court papers, taught English as a Second Language, and even shared my love of dance with others. For many, I was the first detainee they met. As a house mouse, I taught them how to respond to count times, distance themselves from deputies, and address each respectably with Ma'am or Sir.

I became close to many of the officers as well. Most were amazingly patient, funny, and helpful. They would call me if they suspected something or knew someone was feeling down.

The day after my bond hearing, I called my uncle. My previous judge was notorious for denying bonds, which typically resulted in self-deportation. Nevertheless, I chose not to give up.

"Hello," my uncle answered the phone call.

"Hi Uncle, how are you?" I am good, he replied, and he sounded excited. "Everything is set," he said.

"What?" I answered. The phone connection was good, but I was confused.

"You will be released tomorrow, and I will be there to pick you up," he responded.

I was confused. *Was this real?* It's what I'd always wanted, I thought. *Was it true?* I had to let the news sink in. Then, hearing his excitement, I stood there, shocked. The jail had become my home. I had friends. Detainees, officers, and deputies looked to me for help. I was not ready to leave. I used to think I would be happy when this day came. I would be free to see friends and family again. Filled with excitement, I would jump for joy. But that wasn't how it was.

I was sad, confused, and scared. Jail had become my home. These women were my sisters. I didn't want to say goodbye. Leaving did not make me happy but being free did. These women gave my life purpose. They showed me the power of humility and service and made me better.

"Hello, Grace? Are you still there?" my uncle asked.

"I, yes, I'm sorry. Okay." Shocked, I hung up the phone, and as soon as I did, a small group of women rushed up to me, wanting to know the news. They knew what was happening.

"I'm leaving," I muttered. They cheered. I continued... "tomorrow."

"Girl, you have been here too long." "Way too long." "Forever! Go on and get out of here!" Their excitement made me feel blessed, but somehow everyone knew I would be happier outside, except for me. As I walked to my bunk, some friends looked down. When our eyes met, without knowing, they knew. I was their crutch, and their reactions were what I feared.

News spread fast, and as the hours passed, seemingly everyone wanted to find out what I would do, what I would eat, who I would see, and where I would go when I got out. We asked each other these kinds of questions in the yard when eating lunch or daydreaming. They were empty questions then, things to pass the time. Now they were real questions that begged real answers.

American Asylee

Excited to walk free, I was tempered by the fact that I would walk alone. They would remain there, waiting. Created from tragedy behind concrete walls, my asylum-seeking sisters had a bond more powerful than the ocean I came from. I prayed these relationships would remain for the rest of my life. Some who left before me left letters of hope and encouragement for others. Now it was my turn. I recorded my sisters' booking numbers one by one, each hoping they would get the call I received one day.

My 379th night in jail was the hardest. It was the last time we would make fun of each other, talk about our families, friends, or nothing at all. My final night to write in my journal. I began realizing how much I would miss this place. Here, I met courageous women. Each endured great pain and hardship, hoping for a better future for themselves and their children. I would hear "goodnight" the last night in so many different languages. I was so blessed to know these amazing women who together mustered bits of joy in our fight for asylum.

***

The next morning felt like any other morning until I remembered it was my last day in jail. Excited, sad, and flooded with every different feeling on the emotional spectrum, I waited for deputies to call me for the final count. I would change into my bright green, jail-issued suit, fix my bed, and stand for inspection one more time. My messy hair made the deputy giggle as she passed.

I walked on a cloud filled with emotions the whole day. *Was tonight really going to happen? Would I never sleep in my block again? Would I never be surrounded by these sisters again?* It felt surreal. Deputies asked what I would do once out. I had no clue. They laughed. I'd been here for so long; I stopped thinking about leaving.

After dinner, friends asked me to dance one last time before leaving. However, the yard where we typically danced was closed. Dancing inside the facility was against the rules. But, since it was my last night, I asked for special permission. With permission, I danced one last hula, their favorite.

As I moved, I watched their eyes. Some smiled, and others cried. My heart broke further with each step. So unforgettable, it was the saddest dance I ever danced. Everyone clapped when I finished, and I made my way around the room, saying goodbye to each person. The deputies called my number to report for release. My friends gathered my belongings with me and walked me to the door.

One buzz, one click, one turn. I walked through, looking back the entire way. The deputy took me to a room. "Change fast. Your bus is almost here," she said and placed a brown bag at my feet. Inside were the clothes I came to jail in. I reached in, pulled out my maroon tennis shoes, black pants, and a blue shirt. It was the last time I would take off the green uniform. I was amazed and confused. After changing, I waited outside. Finally, the bus arrived with friends just returning from court. I was so happy to see them.

"Are you leaving?" one asked as she passed. "Look Away! Stop talking!" the deputy barked. As she passed, I whispered, "Yes." I walked towards the bus that would take me out of jail, climbed the steps, and took my seat. As the bus moved, I looked back. Again, I whispered, *what an experience!*

I walked to the counter to sign my release papers. Thinking I would be a flight risk, they put an ankle monitor on me for three months. *This will be interesting,* I thought. The officer asked which ankle I wanted it on. I extended my right foot.

Can I shower with it, I asked?

"Yes, of course, the device is waterproof. You can shower and swim with it, but we don't recommend going to the beach with it because sand can damage the equipment." He explained what I could and could not do, where I could and couldn't go. To me, it sounded like I was still incarcerated. I lifted my leg. It was heavy. It was my reminder—though free, I was still in detention.

My uncle met me at the facility entrance. He was so happy to see me. I was glad to see him, but my heart was still with my sisters. He gave me his phone to call my mom and tell her I was no longer in jail.

"I'm so happy, but at the same time so sorry you had to go through that," she said.

I told her how great of an experience it was.

"Did they give you something over there, like drugs... or something? You don't sound like my Grace. How could an American jail be a great experience?"

I laughed. *No, mum, they were lovely, and everything is okay.* Relieved and glad to finally hear my voice, we made plans to talk once at my uncle's home.

A new purpose

The ankle monitor was a challenge to navigate. It rattled against walls when I walked. It was something new I had to get used to. It's weight. It's stigma. It was my unflattering accessory, courtesy of ICE and Orange County. Though happy to be out, I was still in jail.

To answer all the questions my fellow detainees asked. The first person I called was my mom. I went to San Pedro, and my first meal was fish. My uncle prepared salmon with his special sauce and, of course, rice. I can't describe how it felt tasting fish again, other than saying it tasted like freedom. I ate what I wanted, and it was great! The smell and taste took me back home, a place that remained in my heart but never this close to my mind. Savoring each bite, I was thankful.

I missed my asylum-seeking sisters. All I talked about over dinner was how bad I felt knowing they were still in jail. The following day I didn't feel like going anywhere. I was embarrassed. I had been chained, handcuffed, and now monitored. I was an American Asylee, a criminal. Visible to everyone but me, it was hard to see the bright side. I was finally free. I had fish in my belly and rice in the cupboard. Was this not enough to wipe away the shame and remorse I felt?

I spent the first two weeks at home. Limited only to a certain radius of travel and held to a non-negotiable curfew, it was like jail all over again but a different environment. The worst part of freedom was the ankle monitor. When it buzzed, it shook my whole body. The first time it happened, I was asleep. Thinking I was being returned to jail, I panicked. The battery was low. This happened again at the airport. It buzzed for a good hour and a half before I could replace it. I received a call from immigration that night, reminding me to keep the device charged.

Oddly, boredom came with freedom. In jail, we had structure. We woke up before sunrise; we had chores, meals, responsibilities. But, in my uncle's home, I had no purpose or direction; I just existed.

I planned to start a letter-writing campaign. I knew how powerful letters were, and I wanted to gather support for those still inside. But I needed letter writers. Having a bachelor's degree in Information Science, I knew how to create websites. Building a website was time-intensive and relatively inexpensive, but I had no money and was unemployed.

The process of completing the site was not as easy as I thought. There were many things I had forgotten, and I had to reach out to an old professor for help. He advised me and worked with me to make *dearyous.com*. Too shy to leave the confines of my uncle's apartment, website development consumed all my time and provided me with structure.

Once finished, I decided to approach the Friends of Orange County Detainees for funding. They could help turn my idea into reality. I searched their website for contact information and emailed them explaining my concept. Several days later, I heard back. They were interested and wanted me to attend the next board meeting to present my idea!

Excited, I began researching how to make formal presentations. Research suggested doing things we did in school. But then, school seemed so distant. I thought I wasn't ready. Doubt entered my mind. *Perhaps my sisters were fine without me. Maybe it was better to walk away.* Then, just as I started thinking of giving up, a letter made it to my mailbox. That letter was a sign. It pushed me forward.

I received my work permit in the mail that same day. That week, I began working as a night cleaner. After-hours work suited me; my monitor did not freak people out. It was an excellent place to start, and I earned a small income, which provided me with the means to travel to FOCD's headquarters.

When the meeting began, my palms became sweaty. I sat, nervously awaiting my turn. Finally, I was up. I started by explaining who I was, how I came to know about them, and what I hoped to do for my sisters still in jail. When finished, they asked me about things I hadn't thought about. I could not answer many of their questions and feared losing support. During the questioning, one lady stood up and urged the board to focus on the overarching objective of my project rather than the technical details. Ultimately, they agreed my idea had merit, and *dearyous.com* was born. The first task, the "About us" page.

About us

Not many people know that, on any given day, there are up to 34,000 immigrants in detention facilities across the United States. Up to 1,000 immigrants are held in detention facilities in Orange County, California alone. I know because I was one of them. I spent a year and two weeks inside an immigration detention facility. I was released in 2017. I came to the United States due to the extreme domestic violence I experienced on my small island. I went to the United States to find freedom and a peaceful life. My experiences inside the detention facility were among the most rewarding in my life. This may sound crazy since I was incarcerated, but I was able to find joy and satisfaction through serving others on the inside. I had never had so many opportunities to help others until I was placed in jail.

I started by teaching basic English to a small group of women who had never attended school before. They wanted to use their time in jail to learn. I continued to seek out more opportunities to help others in jail. This gave me a new direction, a life that was no longer about me, a life now dedicated to serving others who desperately needed someone because they did not have anybody else.

I created this letter-writing service because it is hard inside when you face trials and challenges alone. To have at least one person on the outside who is willing to encourage and support you means the world. Receiving a letter was one of my favorite moments while in jail. It always made my day better. Finally, someone outside knew I existed and took the time to write to me. Even just half a page brought a smile to my face and lifted my spirits. However, it made me sad to see many women never receiving anything. Either their families were not in the United States, or the families in their home countries could not send a letter. Remembering the women who did not receive any mail is why I created this website. I wanted to provide an opportunity for people to write detainees in their free time.

Additionally, receiving documents for the court is a massive problem for detainees since it takes so long for international mail to arrive from their home countries. Waiting on documentation meant having to push back their court dates, prolonging the time in jail. These simple things may seem like they aren't a big deal, or it doesn't matter, but it matters to detainees. It would mean the world to them to know that there is someone out there willing to offer their service or even one heart willing to provide love and care.

It would mean the world to me if you could tell others about my website, initiative, and anyone else you feel may benefit from my letter-writing service. *Thank you!*

***

Ten days after my release, I turned thirty-one, and my Los Angeles family decided to take me out to a Thai restaurant to celebrate. Before dinner, my cousin took me to a hair salon. After a year in jail, my hair needed serious attention. Despite wearing an ankle monitor, I was genuinely grateful for all they did for me on my 31st birthday. Eventually, I became less embarrassed by the monitor. I would not let it define me, and if people judged me, it was okay; they didn't know my story. I was more than grateful for the support I received from my Los Angeles family and decided not only to see the best in my situation but live each day for my sisters still behind bars.

Christmas 2018

★ ★ ★

I'd been writing drafts of this book for months and had just finished an outline of "Christmas in Jail" when the idea of a Christmas in jail, part 2, came to mind. I wanted to be the one on the outside who made Christmas happen. A friend took an interest in what I was doing and wanted to make a short video.

Most detainees in the facility spoke Spanish. If she wanted to film participants, I would need to find people who could write Christmas letters in Spanish. The first place that came to mind was a Spanish-speaking ward in my church. Since I was not a ward member, I worried they might question my motive. I began doubting myself, but dwelling on doubt did not help.

After church, I looked for leaders with connections. I approached one lady connected with the Spanish ward and asked if she knew leaders in the congregation. Without hesitation, she gave me a phone number. Excited, I reached out that afternoon.

Through text, I introduced myself and what I was hoping to do. The following day, as I prepared for work, my phone vibrated. Her message read:

> I was trying to think of a Christmas activity that would be meaningful for my women, and you just gave me an idea! So let me know what I need to do, and I'll schedule the letter-writing event.

I couldn't believe it. I was more than excited! How could I explain the enormity of their kindness? I read her message ten times and thanked God for putting everything in place. It had been months since I gave back to my sisters, which did not sit well with me. However, this event would reconnect me with my purpose.

If these people were willing to write letters at the drop of a hat, surely, I could find people to make Christmas happen for my sisters. In my mind, I was brought back to Christmas in jail. We didn't have much, but what we had, we shared. So simple, it meant everything to everyone. Could I replicate it? Who would I send the money to?

The facility was too far from where I lived, but my friend had a car and was willing to take me back. She even made a video of me going back since it was my first time returning. Once past security, I waited for the shuttle to take me to the facility. Waiting, I looked over the names on the list. Finally, my eyes fixed on Blessing. When it was time, Blessing approached me with the biggest smile. I was thrilled. "I am so grateful that you chose to visit me," she said.

We started talking about things both of us liked. I shared that I was imprisoned in the same facility. She was surprised. After the first five minutes, I felt she was the right person to give a Christmas contribution. She couldn't believe it. I gathered the money needed and sent it. Weeks later, I received a thank you note from her.

Dear Grace,

I cannot explain how grateful I am to have you as my friend. You can't imagine the joy you put in my heart the day you came to visit. It is heartwarming to know that someone who does not know me can care so much. Ever since the day you came, you have given me strength. Being the first person you have visited makes me feel so blessed. You have such a sweet and beautiful soul. Wanting to help people you don't even know shows you are a good person.

Thank you so much for the money. Even though it came after Christmas, we are planning something big for New Year's Eve. Thanks to you, we bought many things from the commissary. So many who have nothing will at least have something to eat with others on that day.

Christmas was great! We celebrated just how you told me you did when you were here. When the yard opened, we went out to sing and dance. Some deputies danced with us! It was awesome. Though we didn't have anything to share that day, we had a wonderful time. I will still write to you after the New Year. Thanks so much for being such a blessing to us. May God bless you with a splendid holiday!

Blessing!

A month after the celebration, Blessing was released on bond, and like me, awaits her trial.

Déjà vu?

★ ★ ★

On the outside, learning new skills, having new responsibilities, and getting paid for work was exciting! I filed paperwork, counted/deposited rents, adjusted insurance coverages, and oversaw property repair requests in my uncle's rental business. The job was easy, convenient, and routine. I saw it as a first step towards living my American dream. However, after a year, I wanted more. I wanted to live on my own. To do this, I needed more than a part-time job.

I had a friend who worked at Los Angeles International airport, where I was arrested. Her office was looking to hire more people for front-end operations. This was my chance, I thought! I worked on my resume and application when she sent me the information. If I wanted to move forward with American life, I had to land a full-time position. Surprisingly, I was called for an interview one day after applying. Three days later, I was called for a second interview. Within a week, I was offered a position.

Putting on my uniform for the first time was interesting. The long-sleeved white blouse, dark blue pants, and black shoes reminded me of a school uniform. I was thrilled not to worry about what to wear to work each day.

Before leaving for my first day of work, I checked my bag to ensure I didn't forget anything; my employee badge, nametag, scarf…check! Even though I had no idea how to tie my scarf, I tried my best. Arriving as an LAX employee was different. Even though I had been there countless times before as a traveler and was arrested once, I was now part of the LAX team.

I stood across from the Philippines Airline counter, wearing my uniform and badge, thinking how unreal this was. The other woman hired with me, Nancy, was waiting at the counter. Equally excited, she seemed more put together than I. I asked if she could help me with mine. She laughed and said, "I have no idea. I just tied it onto my neck." Both of us laughed as an employee approached. "Welcome, my name is Johanna! Are you ready for your first day?" Both of us eagerly shook our heads. "Great! Follow me!" she said.

Our first order of business was learning how to tie our scarves. There was a particular folding and tying method we practiced repeatedly. "Trust me. You will get used to it," she said. Both of us stared at each other with blank faces as we tried with little to no luck. Soon, other employees began entering the small office and introducing themselves to us before running to the check-in counters. The day went by fast and became more hectic by the minute. I loved the new environment, the job, and the interactions with all the people. It was vastly different from what I became used to at the rental agency.

***

In my second week, I was assigned to the arrivals area and was responsible for the deportation and detainment of passengers. I stepped back into the room that changed my life forever. Even though I worked at LAX, the room terrorized me. I remembered waiting there for agents to decide my fate. I worried that I would be deported to the country I fled.

As I walked in, everything came back. My heart raced. I was hot and felt dizzy. After three years, nothing changed. The only thing that had was who I had become. As I looked at those detained, not knowing who they were there, my heart sank. I knew what was going through their minds.

FEAR.

Taking their details, I felt their panic. Voices trembled as they spelled their names. An officer entered. "No cell phones allowed," he commanded. I remembered that tone. It was hard for me to stay. Even though I wasn't them, I saw myself in their eyes—next, the deportation room. I spent hours waiting there for my deportation. Still cold, still only one thin blanket.

FLASHBACKS.

Three years after my detainment experience, these immigration officers are now colleagues. Emotions confused every part of my being. I stepped out of the room and walked away. I wondered if this would get easier. I knew I needed to let my past go and focus on my present. I knew the officers were doing their jobs, and I did my best to do mine. Several days later, I was again assigned to the rooms. Focusing on my present, I went back in. My past gave me the ability to empathize with those in the rooms. I showed compassion, doing all I could to let them know I was there for them, even if just for a few minutes. It was all I could do.

PURPOSE.

A new beginning

★ ★ ★

Residing with my uncle, I commuted to and from the airport for four-hour split shifts. The commute was long, sometimes taking up to three hours. For weeks, I would leave at 4 am only to return at 2 am the following day. Two hours of rest between shifts was not enough. I knew I had to do something. I planned on finding a place closer to the airport and possibly live with roommates to ease rent. I had never lived on my own before, but I had to move closer to the airport if I wanted to keep my job.

My co-workers convinced me to find a place of my own. I feared not being financially stable and living paycheck to paycheck. What savings I had was not enough. I had never saved money before. Whatever I had was remitted to help my family back home. Living on my own meant an abrupt end to remittances.

All my credit cards were maxed out, and I only had a couple of hundred dollars to my name. If I were to move out, I would have to work as many hours as possible to make rent. I wondered if I wanted too much, too fast. Would I be better off staying with my uncle? I decided leaving was best.

Searching for a place close to the airport between shifts was difficult. I gave myself three days to explore the area, and on the third day, I found a place minutes from work. It was a home owned by an older couple from the Philippines with an in-law unit. They responded quickly to my application, and I had my place. I couldn't wait to move in.

I felt accomplished the day I picked up my keys. Moments like these were as rare as cold days in Kiribati. Things were finally coming together. At 32 years of age, I had my first place.

One week after moving in, I caught shingles. The pain forced me to miss an entire week of work. At that time, my health was not a priority; money was. I worried about the following month's rent more than anything. I used all my savings for the security deposit and my first month's rent. I needed to work.

Desperately, I investigated all my credit card balances. I discovered a new charge of over a thousand dollars I didn't recognize. *How did this happen?* I tried not to panic, but it was no use. *Maybe I shouldn't have moved out.* I had no direction or purpose other than to survive. Staring blankly at my ceiling, I fell asleep, hoping for a better tomorrow.

***

It wasn't bad enough that I was sick and broke. I had an appointment at the Immigration office the following day. I needed to check in since I missed my hearing. I walked into the room filled with others who had ankle monitors. Some hid the devices with baggy pants or long skirts, while others with shorts left them out for all to see. I checked in and asked the lady at the front if she knew what would happen.

"Full name, please." She entered my information. "You've been here before?" Embarrassed, I nodded. "Give me a minute to find out who your officer is. We rarely bring people back here," she said.

I worried and called my immigration officer. "Grace, you are lucky," he said.

Lucky? I questioned. I took a deep breath, prepared myself for incarceration, and listened.

"We've been trying to contact you, but you didn't answer your phone. Because of that, the agency decided not to default and give you another chance. But since we couldn't get a hold of you, ICE decided to move to the next step and affix another ankle monitor on you." To me, the punishment fit. So I accepted the penalty and was cuffed again.

Staring at the monitor on the bus ride home, I wondered what to do now. Illness took me out of work for a week. I maxed out all my credit cards. I had no savings, and worst of all, no one to talk to. I was entirely lost.

I sent an email explaining my circumstances and asked if there was any way I could still work with my monitor. Immediately my supervisor responded, saying I could still work, and they would accommodate my situation. With work sorted, I called the company that charged my credit card. Call after the call; no one was willing to drop the charges. Again, I sent emails, and just when I was about to give up, I received an email response granting a full refund. Things were beginning to turn around.

Missing home

— ★ ★ ★ —

I*t's been four years since I left home*, I thought as I waited for my 2:00 a.m. Uber. When I moved closer to the airport, I asked for as many hours as possible. I was chasing money, going home only to shower and sleep. The more I reflected on what my life had become, the more I realized how lonely it was.

The road was so quiet, and the sky so clear. The few stars scattered throughout the sky had no impact on the ground under my feet. I remembered the village at that moment. The light illuminated everything; the dirt path leading home, palm tree shadows, and ghostly smatterings from galactical heavens above. The little bit of light from the sky barely lit the white lines on the road. There were not many cars in Lot E that night. I rechecked my phone to see where my Uber was — like a slow-moving Pac-man, three minutes away.

It had been weeks since I visited my San Pedro family. I missed them more than they knew. Living on my own was tough. My apartment was convenient but expensive. I worked six days a week, and on my day off, I stayed home to do housework. Of highest importance was cleaning my uniform. I had two blazers, two scarves, five shirts, one pair of pants, and one skirt. Keeping myself busy detracted the loneliness I felt.

Some days, check-in responsibilities depressed me. I saw people traveling home and got jealous. How lucky and blessed they were to go back. Weighing their boxes full of souvenirs and candies for families always made me wish I could have done the same. So often, I wished I were them. Watching people say goodbye at the airport every day constantly reminded me of my last goodbyes.

The day before I left Kiribati, I said my final goodbye to my mom. She was not able to drop me off at the airport. Kiribati is a small country where everyone knows everything—having her at the airport would start gossip, spreading like wildfire. I didn't want anyone to know I was leaving. I was scared and ashamed. Ashamed that my second marriage had failed, embarrassed that I couldn't take the abuse like so many other women back home do, embarrassed that I would stain my family's name more than I already had. I bid her farewell the day before I left.

Abused by my father, she stayed in her marriage. Me? I ran away. I felt like I was betraying my husband, and my actions proved I didn't love him. But the truth is, I did love him. So I tried convincing my mom to allow me to give him another chance.

"Grace, you've given him opportunity after opportunity, and see what that got you? You lost your baby, and you almost lost your life in that hospital. Think about your life. What use is it if you're dead under his hands? Think about the women who are also being abused here, thinking there's no way out. If you leave your husband, you will show them that there is a way and that staying in an abusive relationship is not right. Leaving does not dishonor you. Leaving is honorable for you and for us, the ones who stayed. I could not leave. You are stronger. Leaving is what you must do."

She always knew what I needed to hear. I decided to leave for myself and all abused women in Kiribati.

Becoming alien

--- ★ ★ ★ ---

Alien / ˈālēən/: 1. coming from a different country, race, or group: 2. strange and not familiar: 3. relating to creatures from another planet. The word / ˈālēən/ defines things that do not belong.

Invisibly tattooed on my skin is my A number, #531161498. I'm an alien. I don't belong here. I remember seeing strange and scary aliens in movies when I was little. The good guys with guns rid societies of aliens and saved everyone from outside invasions. In my case, it is the same. I do not belong here. Good guys with guns protect America from asylees. Good guys with guns keep us out. Good guys with guns locked me up. I am an alien, and I should be sent back to where I escaped.

Attached to my A number is my personal information, date of entry, claim status, location, American contacts, health, everything. As an asylee, the only thing needed is my A number. Back home, I was Grace; here, I am, #531161498.

American Asylee

The word alien didn't bother me until a coworker approached me. "So, what's your status? Are you a citizen? Permanent resident? What are you?" I thought about it. Were those the only options? What about asylum seekers? I did not fit her boxes. I did not have a status.

I am seeking asylum, I said. Her face, paralyzed in a perplexing state of confused disapproval, made me feel even more of an outcast than I already did. It seemed most American citizens didn't recognize asylum seekers. *It's more of a liminal existence than anything else,* I said. *What I mean is, I am standing in line waiting for my case to be heard, waiting to start a life of my own. I've been waiting for three years.*

"What do you mean," she asked.
I don't have a status yet, I replied, *but I have a work permit.*
"Oh," she said, then walked away.

Perpetually having others question my existence made me question it myself. Was it worth it? To stay and fight for asylum, fight for forgiveness? Fight for mercy? Fight for acceptance in a place I did not belong? I felt ashamed of my status in a home where I had no name. This was ridiculous! I wanted to live in a country that did not want me, and the more I thought about it, the greater my frustration. I could not do anything. I had to wait. No matter how badly I wanted to take control, I couldn't. My life rested in the hands of others.

A week later, I received an email from my lawyer, reminding me about my upcoming court date. Finally, finally, it's here, I thought, hoping it would be my first and last court date. It's been a long three years, and now my wait is finally over. In jail, fellow detainees always joked about waiting. They said it was sexy. To me, it was scary, especially if you don't know what you're waiting for.

Entering through an armed entrance, I walked into the courthouse. Other detainees and families watched as I placed my hands on the wall for frisking. I tried to remind myself not to be embarrassed since I was not a *real* criminal. My uncle let me know everyone else had to go through the same process when I sat next to him.

After a few minutes, our lawyer arrived. She apologized for being late and quickly went over my case proceedings. The officer called my alien number to stand before the judge when finished.

The courtroom was different. It was not crowded. I was not shackled. My bright green jumpsuit was replaced by more formal attire. It was my first time seeing this judge.

Are you fluent in English?
Yes.
So, you don't need a translator?
No.

The judge explained that we would need to restart my case since the first judge left no notes from previous appearances. Then, with nothing else to discuss, she wrote down a date, April 14, 2022, and instructed us to return then.

Court is adjourned. That was it.

I slowly walked out of the courtroom and thought to myself, *three more years, I'll remain #531161498.*

American Asylee

Dismayed, we left

with a trinket of hope,

at the foot of a doorstep

for all to see

the strength,

and the power

of this American Asylee.

COVID-19

— ★ ★ ★ —

IT was valentine's day when I received the news. I'd been waiting for this ever since I walked away from the interview. Finally, American Airlines offered the position. I was super excited, like when I received my offer from Philippines Airlines. Except, this time, I was more confident having years of experience in the airline industry. I couldn't keep the news to myself. I had to share it with everyone I knew.

A new sense of freedom washed over me as I began imagining traveling through flight benefits. I started listing the states I wanted to visit, things I wanted to do, and people I hoped to see. For me, getting a job at American was one more step towards my American dream.

Around the same time, a family member asked for my assistance finding a new place to live. As we researched, we could not find any affordable place. I decided to move in with her to help pay for a home together. In March, we found a two-bedroom apartment with a large living room. The location was perfect. I couldn't help but laugh at myself as I began packing my little studio so close to the airport. I was so proud to be living on my own and remember thinking the studio would be my place for a long time. In retrospect, though, the most challenging part of March was not the move; it was the coronavirus.

Managers began talking about coronavirus and disrupted flight schedules in Asia. At first, it seemed like it was the same kind of news we were all used to; flights were delayed or canceled. But, the following day, our manager told us how the virus was spreading rapidly in Asia and if uncontrolled, we may lose flights.

That same week I received a call from American alerting me that onboarding with the company would not proceed because of the virus. As a result, they had to lay off staff and freeze hiring. Soon, the Philippines went into lockdown, canceling all flights. Later that month, Los Angeles went into lockdown.

When locked down began, people panicked. Grocery stores were filled with shoppers shopping as if the world would end. Desperate and nervous, everyone was in panic mode—long lines, social distancing, and masks everywhere. My cousins and I went shopping to ensure a long-term food and water supply. While our focus was on food, everyone else's seemed to be on toilet paper. Every store ran out of toilet paper early on, and entrepreneurial minds quickly seized the opportunity. Soon, street corners had pop-up stands selling sanitizer and toilet paper with considerable markups.

The numbers dying from the virus increased with each passing minute, and for that reason, I ignored TVs and radio stations. I knew the virus was serious, but I didn't want constant reminders of the death chamber we were living in. Most of the deaths were elderly. Coworkers took leave because they had extended family to care for. Soon after, our company followed all other airlines and began laying off workers. Suddenly, one of the busiest airports in the world was void of people. It was weird. Without people or flights, I soon would find myself without income.

On top of rent and food, I had just started car payments for my new Toyota Prius. Fortunately, I qualified for a portion of my company's unemployment fund. It temporarily covered expenses. I began looking for other opportunities. I worked for Instacart, briefly sold life insurance, and began a small T-shirt design business for extra income.

Kiribati closed its borders early in 2020 to nonessential travel and did not have immediate plans to reopen its borders. Thankfully, this move prevented COVID from reaching Kiribati. However, seafarers staying in shelters, hotels, and homestays in various parts of the world have been trapped abroad for over a year.

American Asylee

Months after halting international flights, Philippine Air Lines resumed limited transport. Before the pandemic, two flights a day came from Manilla: now, only one. To make it fair, all employees worked rationed shifts. Despite fewer hours, all were thankful and hopeful for a quick return to normal operations. Since I had a vehicle, commuting to work was easier. At first, the freeway was empty. The city was a skeleton of what it used to be as people worked remotely. Cars on the highway were sparse.

In April, I received a letter from American Airlines. Flights were returning to normal operations, and my work permit was about to expire. So, a week after beginning my onboarding process with American Airlines, I resigned from Philippines Airlines.

I notified American Airlines of my delayed work permit during my second week. I was instructed to get an update from UCIS and follow up with human resources. Unfortunately, due to COVID, UCIS extended work permit processing times from 3-6months to 8-11 months. Therefore, I needed to have patience and wait.

Patience and waiting were the two things I didn't have or want to do, but I knew I had no choice. I explained everything to American Airlines human resources, and I was granted three months of unpaid work leave and promised a job when I received work authorization. I completed my first two weeks of training on July 22, 2021, before taking a forced sabbatical.

It was then I realized I'd been holding back from completing American Asylee. Somehow everything in the pandemic pushed me to finish our story. Is this the end? Or the beginning? The idea of freedom is a constant struggle between mind and body. And, though our bodies were incarcerated, our minds were not. America gives us the right to fight for freedom, the right to tell our stories. But, if detained, our minds can't follow.

Tina, Solange, Ale, Juliet, Martha, and countless other asylees like us, incarcerated through violence, fighting for freedom, and set free by hope. We have traveled too far, cried too long, and lost more than we'd ever imagined. Yet, we can't give up. These are our trials. These are our stories.

You are our hope.
Thank you!

An escape plan

★ ★ ★

Before ending my story, I wanted to share the steps I took to escape domestic violence. I hope that these steps can be of use to anyone seeking an escape from a situation that seems impossible.

1. **Turn to others:** Sharing what I was experiencing made all the difference. Keeping my truth to myself would have killed me. Sharing with others lightened my burden and led to a plan for escape. At first, I did not want to tell others about my problems. I thought doing so would be selfish. *Everyone has issues; why share mine?* Sometimes it takes others to show you what you don't want to see. I had to lose my baby and almost my life before gaining the courage to leave. Don't wait until it's too late. There are people in your life ready to help. Stop assuming the worst and start believing in yourself. Believe in others. As you open yourself to others, you will find a way out.

2. **Have courage:** You are strong. Leaving is not easy. You have lived with pain for too long. The person you

once loved would never harm you the way you have been. There is no easy way out. You need to stand up for yourself. Every life is a gift from God, and one should not endanger another. We are all created for extraordinary purposes. The fact that you are still breathing means your mission in life is not finished. Learn from your past. Move forward. You are worth fighting for.

3. **Focus on the positive:** It may not be an easy decision, but we both know it's the best decision. So, focus on the positive, and you'll find courage.

4. **Plan, move forward, don't look back:** Planning is essential. If you have children, talk to them. Include them in your plan. They may not want to leave, but they must for their safety. If he can abuse you, he can abuse them. Ready a safe place. It could be a friend's house, a women's shelter, or your own family's residence. Prepare cash for emergencies. Leaving is safer when you have means. You will have more confidence to escape. I fled to another country. It was scary, but it was possible with preparation and help from others.

5. **Let God take care of the rest:** God will do the rest once we do our part. He sees what you cannot see. He

knows what you do not know. We can't expect God to do everything for us, and we can't do everything on our own. As bad as it was, the abusive relationship made me realize that with God's help, I was stronger than my husband.

6. **Know who you are:** Knowing who you are plays a pivotal role. As the daughter of a great God, you hold great power to withstand more than you ever thought you could. You are talented and unique. Never let anyone decide your worth. God created you to be precious and beautiful, no matter what you have endured. You are his most precious treasure. Don't ever forget that.

7. **Laugh:** There is something about laughter that makes everything better. Laughter lightens some of our heaviest burdens. Laughter brings joy, and when shared, creates closeness with others. After my first husband left, many asked what had happened. I understood their curiosity, but it seemed harsh. So I answered their questions with humor: *I like my marriages like I like my men, short.*

8. **Let go:** Sometimes, we hold onto people because of memories. My broken marriages left me with many grievances. I blamed others for my problems. The

minute I decided to let go was when I found my freedom. I chose to live happily in my here and now, no longer living in the past.

9. **Forgive:** Holding on to grudges never helps. You lose control of everything, and before you know it, there seems no way out. Forgiveness brings healing to both the forgiver and forgiven.

10. **Accept what you can't control and move forward:** Before the final decree was signed, my first husband disclosed his true feelings for his ex. Not thinking that his feelings would impact our marriage, he married me. Too often, accepting the uncontrollable requires sacrifice. If we remained married, I would have been miserable competing with her. So instead, I allowed what I could not control to happen and moved on.

Gratitude Journal

★ ★ ★

This Journal Belongs To

You can complain because rose bushes have thorns or rejoice that thorn bushes have roses. It's all how you look at it.

J. Kenfield Morley

Recall a favorite memory that you're grateful for

_____

_____

_____

_____

_____

Good things that happened today

_____

_____

_____

_____

_____

The struggle ends when the gratitude begins.
Neale Donald Walsh

What painful experience has helped you grow?

_____

_____

_____

_____

_____

Lessons I learned today

_____

_____

_____

_____

_____

Gratitude paints little smiley faces on everything it touches.

Richelle E. Goodrich

Make a list of 10 things that always make you smile

_____

_____

_____

_____

_____

Good things that happened today

_____

_____

_____

_____

_____

Gratitude makes sense of your past, brings peace for today, and creates a vision for tomorrow
Melody Beattie

What's something you're grateful for today that you didn't have a year ago?

_____

_____

_____

_____

_____

Lessons learned today

_____

_____

_____

_____

_____

American Asylee

Gratitude turns what we have into enough.

Aesop

Write about a friend that you're grateful for

_____

_____

_____

_____

_____

Good things that happened today

_____

_____

_____

_____

_____

It's not happiness that brings us gratitude. It's gratitude that brings us happiness.
Anonymous

What's one of the personality traits that you're grateful for?

_____

_____

_____

_____

_____

Lessons I learned today

_____

_____

_____

_____

_____

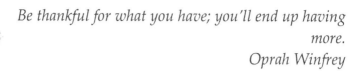

Be thankful for what you have; you'll end up having more.
Oprah Winfrey

How are you able to help others?

_____

_____

_____

_____

_____

Good things that happened today

_____

_____

_____

_____

_____

The invariable mark of wisdom is to see the
miraculous in the common.
Ralph W Emerson

What everyday object are you grateful for?

_____

_____

_____

_____

_____

Lessons I learned today

_____

_____

_____

_____

_____

Gratitude is riches; complaint is poverty.
Doris Day

What is your favorite treat?

_____

_____

_____

_____

_____

Good things that happened today

_____

_____

_____

_____

_____

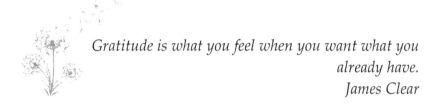

Gratitude is what you feel when you want what you already have.
James Clear

Recall a time when you received a compliment; what about it made you grateful?

_____

_____

_____

_____

_____

Lessons I learned today

_____

_____

_____

_____

_____

The root of joy is Gratefulness.
David Steindl-Rast

What holiday tradition are you most thankful for?

_____

_____

_____

_____

_____

Good things that happened today

_____

_____

_____

_____

_____

Gratitude is a powerful catalyst for happiness.
It's the spark that lights a fire of joy in your soul.
Amy Collette

What do you think about when you can't sleep?

_____

_____

_____

_____

_____

Lessons I learned today

_____

_____

_____

_____

_____

American Asylee

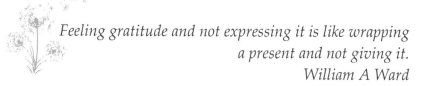

Feeling gratitude and not expressing it is like wrapping
a present and not giving it.
William A Ward

Name your favorite childhood memory

_____

_____

_____

_____

_____

Good things that happened today

_____

_____

_____

_____

_____

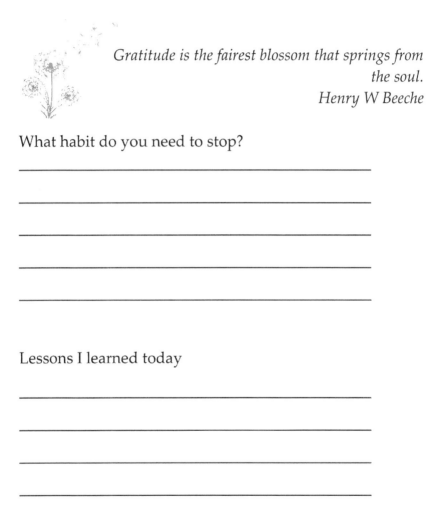

Gratitude is the fairest blossom that springs from
the soul.
Henry W Beeche

What habit do you need to stop?

_____

_____

_____

_____

_____

Lessons I learned today

_____

_____

_____

_____

_____

...

I believe history is made by people who try. Successful or not, these people tried. Imagine if everyone who had a story to tell gave up before telling it. Where would our world be today if they all gave up? I have a story to tell, and I won't give up because I am an immigrant — I don't know how to give up.

- Grace James